STR[illegible]

FO[illegible]

BIRDS

Birding Verses and Puzzles

by

Frank Dobinson

Published by:

DOBINSON
BARNSTAPLE DEVON

First printed in Great Britain, 1995

ISBN 0 9526905 0 0

Printed in Great Britain by
Arthur H. Stockwell Ltd.
Elms Court Ilfracombe
Devon

FOREWORD

My serious interest in birds began in the seventies, though, possibly, the seeds were sown many years ago when my father used to take us, brothers and sisters, out for country walks. That was when I first heard the phrase "A little bit of bread and no cheese" applied to the song of a Yellowhammer.

I hope bird-watchers will find the contents amusing, which is my primary intention, and will forgive the many puns. Here and there a new word has been coined where it seems to fit the situation.

I am aware of changing bird nomenclature in the UK, so that some references are, now, no longer strictly valid. This applies particularly to some lines in the Ontario pieces. However I have decided to leave the text as written a year or two ago.

I must thank the many birders, wardens and rangers, members of the RSPB, and county societies in the South East, the South West, and some folk abroad, for their friendship and help in widening my knowledge of such a fascinating hobby. In particular, I wish to mention the Torridge Branch of the Devon Bird-watching and Preservation Society.

F.A.D. 1995

In memory of my late wife, Kathleen,
for her patience and forbearance.

CONTENTS

SPECIES

GANNETS

Right across the world, they span it,
In most corners of the planet,
Quite prolific bird the Gannet,
Fishing several oceans.

Sociable breeder, crowding rock,
Small space taking enormous flock,
Can decimate the sea fish stock,
Renowned voracious feeder.

If at a coastline you arrive,
Watch for Gannets, and watch them dive,
With folded wings, the sea they rive,
Spectacular immersion.

They're shaped, when seen in silhouette,
More like cigar than cigarette,
Rather than smoked, prefer fish wet,
And hunt it with abandon!

THE GREY HERON

Standing in water, up to your knees,
You don't get rheumatics, you don't even sneeze,
Seen from afar, so grey, black and white,
And it's sooner or later you'll get a bite,
Patiently waiting, ever so still,
Then a lightning move, and that eel's in your bill,
It writhes and wriggles but cannot slip
Away from that formidable clenching grip;
If there are young for whom you cater,
That catch will he regurgitated later.
To water birds you can be a pest,
You're not above snatching a chick from its nest,
Whole Gull colony jumps from the ground,
They will chase you away, should you come around.
It's not Heron-eous, no, to say,
That horticultural goldfish can fall prey;
Such drastic ills need cures as drastic,
Some gardeners have faith in Herons plastic,
Laid back in flight, that bend to the neck,
Do you get a crick? Does it hurt when you peck?
Cruising along on that outsize wing,
There's that guttural call, you surely can't sing.
Hanging around inland or on coast,
Ardea cinerea, hardier than most,
In lowest temp'ratures dramatic,
Looking for creatures inviting aquatic.
Early nest in tree tops, side by side
So massive the structure, so deep and so wide,
Annu'lly added to, branch and stick,
Rising like a tower block, brick upon brick,
Such great arboreal emplacement
Can provide a des res within its basement,
For a much smaller bird who will seek
To be dwelling "out in the sticks" so to speak.

SWANS

Though in all books one is described as Mute,
Yet off its mouth, it has been known to shoot,
Mostly it's said when it's about to die,
Though it will grunt when danger appears nigh,
If under threat great wings come into play,
Menacingly them about it will lay.
The pen will pair with cob throughout their life,
Unchangeable and so faithful a wife,
Notice the neck, how gracefully it's arched,
And the white plumage as though bleached and starched,
Young ones form family circle in the Spring,
Which surely could be called a Cygnet ring!
In wintertime some others will come forth,
The Bewick's, do they motor from the north?
To see a herd of them is quite super,
Even more so in the case of Whooper,
Now which one has feathered its nest? Behold,
It's the Whooper, up front it has more gold!

HONEY BUZZARD

They call it Dartmoor View, it's truly rural,
Panorama of the valley of the Teign,
If time and elements are right
There can occur a splendid sight,
Honey Buzzards, to appear, they sometimes deign.

The Raptor Viewpoint, it's a woodland clearing
It's providing wondrous birding without match,
However be prepared to wait
Until those Buzzards elevate,
And the cry goes up "Look in that third blue patch!"

Now watch those special Raptors when displaying,
In the tail, uniquely barred, a twist to see,
As they ascend in "steps" quite steep,
It's mainly flat wings they will keep,
Then, above, they clap them in *pernistic* glee!

We think one Honey Buzzard's like another,
But variations do occur, that's no yarn,
Though we can't say "See this one here,
It was at Haldon just last year,"
No we certainly cannot, but Robin Khan!

Not a Buteo but it's most impressive,
Honey Buzzard, we expect that it would seize
Large prey, not insects for its fare
But dig out wasps' nests it will dare,
It will honeycomb the woodland for the bees!

LITTLE RINGED PLOVER

So neat, and so dainty, that comes to mind,
When searching a margin inland, we find,
You and your mate now running, and now still,
Or low on the wing, and calling quite shrill.

But you're not all that careful where you lay
A clutch of four, it's little heed you pay,
Can be on open ground, amongst the stones,
But some will survive and make old bones.

Against predation, a Warden will wage,
By cov'ring the eggs with a large mesh cage,
Frustrating so well the foxes and crows,
And lessening the Little Plover's woes.

Yellow eye ring, will show when seen not far,
Another clue is the absent wing bar,
Legs, unlike orange of the Ringed, are pale,
All helping to distinguish without fail.

Charadrius dubius? Why the doubt?
The previous verse spells differences out
So search with confidence at gravel pit,
There is no need for it, your brow, to knit.

DUNLINS

Of the Calidrids they're most abundant,
Can be approachable, bins redundant;
Such hunched little waders, wheeling away,
Turning in unison, now white, now grey;
Incredibly keeping tight formation,
In an uncolliding integration.
Watch several hundreds, before the flood,
Like sewing machines, they're probing the mud,
And just singly, inland it can be found,
At a reservoir it's often around;
Conspicuous breeding dress they will show
With prominent black belly patch below,
But sometimes recognition is a test,
Some plumages can take time to digest.
Breed on high ground, as ''Alpina'' implies,
Though coastal marshes they may patronise.

REDSHANKS

Rising way off with a shrill "Tew Tew"
The white trailing edges come into view;
In the sun the legs can glow like fire,
Unless they've just stepped in the mire;
Most numerous of the Tringa class,
We soon know if it's too near we pass,
Bobbing the head when it's alerted,
So wary till the risk's averted.
Thick grassy tufts in an open field
Help to keep the clutch of four concealed,
Though not aware of such strict lessons,
That silence won't reveal its presence;
It will, with the neighbours, cruise around
And so advertise its breeding ground.
Awaiting the ebbing of the tide,
When exposed mud bank will soon provide;
Countless marine creatures can fall prey
On what, not for them, could be a good day.
Common Redshank found by the dozen,
Not so the more elusive cousin,
Which has a rarer niche allotted,
Much less observed, though it is Spotted;
Latter one a smarter wader quite,
Distinguished and recognised in flight,
A plain dark wing, no pale edge to it,
And that digestive call of "Chew it".
Often alone, though not always proud,
It will join a Common Redshank crowd,
Where it will stand out, head and shoulders
Above the rest, like books have told us;
Beyond the tail the legs reach well
In flight, and colours we can tell;
So lucky the watchers if they track
One in breeding hue, and "Spot the Black".

GODWITS

Two regular species, here, are sighted,
Bar-tailed and Black-tailed; we'd be excited
Should Marbled or Hudsonian appear,
It would take the crown for many a year.
Quite a picture in breeding cinnamon,
In the Bar-tailed, reaching the abdomen;
Winter, like other waders on the coast,
Godwits assemble, an unnumbered host.
Different jizzes of Bar-tailed and Black,
Distinguishing them, a soon acquired knack,
First take the bills, to differentiate,
The Bar-tailed's upcurved, but the Black-tailed's straight;
If undecided, with bill shape you've failed,
Note the tall elegance of the Black-tailed;
Failing all else, wait till the wings extend,
Then the Black-tailed's white stripe you'll apprehend.
Now it has been said, and here I repeat,
"Godwit" is corruption of "Good to Eat".
There was a time when some folk would scupper
The Godwits for a savoury supper,
And some years ago these birds were shot,
Being considered so good for the pot.
Now, long may they the estuaries enrich,
And their survival suffer no more hitch.

THE CURLEW

Can be often heard, not always seen,
A haunting call from a TV screen,
Picture of moorland, or shore, marine,
Hidden backing group.

Large bird, largest with the Wader tab,
A grotesque long bill, mud flat to stab,
Invertebrate denizens to grab,
Good excavator.

A ground nester, not confined to moor,
Eggs varicoloured, a clutch of four,
In breeding season, insectivore,
The diet to hand.

To coast in winter gravitating,
The estuaries decorating,
In social feed participating,
A low tide menu.

So may it flourish, and stay around,
And wild, open spaces still abound,
So we yet hear the engaging sound,
That "Cour-li, Cour-li".

SNIPES

Birds of the marsh, the Common one's found
All the year, it's a resident kind,
When displaying, as it dives to ground,
Its tail feathers make that bleating sound
In an effort, its mate, to spellbind.

But the Jack Snipe's much harder to pick,
Only wintering here, in the reeds,
It has a most unusual trick,
Bobbing as though on a pogo stick,
And it's performing this while it feeds.

More sighting headaches to countervail,
Try examining stripes on the crown,
A central one that's narrow and pale,
Then it's a Common that you can nail,
Wide and dark, that's a Jack, the low-down.

Arctic Summer, Jack will be squatting
In Siberian taiga, it's fine,
When resting quite difficult spotting
But listen for the sound of trotting,
Though, in sight, there'll be nothing equine.

Should a Snipe you get near, and surprise,
Last minute take-off, takes you aback,
But study its movement, how it flies,
Most helpful for you to recognise
Towering Common, or low flight Jack.

PHALAROPES

There's the Grey, the Red-necked, and the Wilson's,
Short stayers as a rule when migrating,
In general they turn up quite near the coast,
Don't miss one, they're so well worth the dating.

Smart and elegant coming to the eye,
With fascination watch the gentle whirl,
Spinning undizzied on water or mud,
And executing a unique pas seul.

We might think them crazy doing their turn,
However they seem to know when to stop,
And that's when it's had the desired effect,
When prey, curious, comes up to the top.

They share a trait with other species, few,
In role reversal, it's their wont to choose,
To have the breeding male bird drably garbed,
And clothe the female in much brighter hues.

And the female's not a normal mother,
For, once the oviparous duties done,
She has no instinct for parental care,
Needless of family she's on the run.

So mother's had enough, she says farewell,
Takes flight, departs, and leaves the breeding shores,
Yielding the nest and the brooding duties,
To father, lumbered with domestic chores.

Such tame, confiding shore-birds as they are,
And inoffensive, so one wonders why
Whenever one appears along our coasts,
It's always manifesting a black eye.

THE BLACK-HEADED GULL

One of the avian misnomers are you,
Since the appelation is scarcely true,
Chocolate the hood, in Summer, you've got,
In Winter reducing to a dark spot,
The wing has attendant white leading edge
And this shows almost as soon as you fledge.
Juvenile's plumage is smart, but nark it,
It isn't a species more up-market!
Uproarious colonies where you nest,
Lifting at times in general protest,
Spec'lly if threatened by thief, or by tide,
Those exposed quarters not easy to hide;
Omnivorous finding food everywhere,
Great opportunist, so well can you fare,
Hard weather, you intensify your quest,
And residential gardens you infest.

KITTIWAKE

Nesting communally, row upon row,
On tall cliffs they share with other sea-birds,
Tiny stepped ledges are where the chicks grow,
How do they survive? One is lost for words;
Precarious home, in that beetling place,
It's so like a noisy tenement block,
There's domestic life on a rough cliff face,
And in it too, they just don't put a sock;
Onomatopoeically calling
"Kitti-wa-ak, Kitti-wa-ak", this they repeat,
Which so many birders find enthralling,
As they watch from a precarious seat.
A most graceful gull to watch in its flight
Over the sea, they keep to the ocean,
Those ink black-tipped wings are a copyright,
And beating ever so fast in motion.

WOOD PIGEONS

Explode from a tree with a mighty thrash,
Blue-grey the colour, and of white a flash,
Single white wing stripes that one can't ignore,
It's the Lance-Jack of the avian corps,
In a flock searching, then down they all drop
To strip a tasty vegetable crop,
Monotonous cooing gives them away,
As perched in a tree, some time they will stay
Raptors are fanciers where they are concerned,
And don't go hungry once the prey's discerned,
Some human fanciers, armed to incommode,
Are drawn to them, so are they pigeon-towed?

THE CUCKOO

The call is so redolent of Spring
It can give pleasure to the ear,
But frightens small birds like anything,
Someone's nest it will commandeer.

First one is reported by letter,
To the paper, *The Times*, no less,
And there can be quite a vendetta
For earliest date in the press.

In reed-bed it's a threat infernal,
No thought of nidification,
And there is no instinct maternal,
That is left to delegation.

It's rather hawk-like in appearance,
But no killer, though it pesters
It will merit the interference
From those threatened little nesters.

The Warbler forgets apprehension,
And becomes a strange egg brooder,
Giving undivided attention
Though it's dwarfed by the intruder.

Now fostered and fledged, the young Cuckoo,
Of parental guidance has none,
Finds its own way to Winter venue,
Flies off to the south for the sun.

Caterpillars they like for their lunch,
And all kinds of noxious grub,
Like the Drinker Moth one, it will munch;
Other birds will quite gladly snub.

THE NIGHTJAR

Down in the forest something churred,
An engine idling that was heard?
Incredibly it was a bird,
The astonishing Nightjar.

When stretched out longwise in a tree,
Almost reptilian it can be,
Well camouflaged, so hard to see,
So barred and streaked all over.

Crepuscular, in faded light,
Above the scrub at no great height,
Obvious can be small patches white,
On angled wings they're showing.

Among moths, havoc it will wreak,
Its other noises help us seek,
Clapping of wings, a wince, a squeak,
Polyphonic performer.

Though insects in nocturnal flight
Are decimated left and right,
Plenty remain that can us bite,
So carry gnat repellent.

THE KINGFISHER

Delight to the eye, despair to the fish,
Blue, green, and chestnut, it's cutting a dash,
Maybe but a glimpse as it speeds away,
Now over the river, gone in a flash.

Sometimes we might catch it at patient rest,
Very still, on a branch overhanging,
Poised ready in piscatorial wait,
A dive follows punctilious scanning.

Emerging straightway, a prize in the bill,
That could be lively, perhaps a small trout,
However it won't be wriggling for long,
Against a bough it will get a good clout.

At times it can be most enterprising,
An angler's rod provides a position,
So making a very contrasting pair,
Ichthyophagists in competition.

In a river bank, in a deep burrow,
Holed up and holding riparian right,
Yes it nests underground which could make it,
Perhaps not a wren, though a troglodyte.

Braving the Winter, and staying around,
Till inland water is iced as it cools,
Then it's off it will go to the seaside,
To sample the menu in the rock pools.

It can be very loud when it's calling,
And ventriloquial tricks it can pull,
It can call to its mate with a whistle,
Even when arriving with its mouth full.

At the end of a birding excursion,
There will be sever'l watchers who will say,
That no matter what ticks are in the book,
The sight of a Kingfisher made their day.

GREEN WOODPECKER

So bright green and yellow, as depicted,
And to *formicide* you are addicted,
Reaching quite deep with that long folding tongue,
A scurry of ants you'll soon be among;
They have no chance when that tongue you protrude,
So you stick to ants as your favourite food;
When disturbed at feeding on the latter
You just treat it as a laughing matter!
And many a grassy surface you've torn
On somebody's so well manicured lawn.
Your flight is quite a diagnostic gait,
As now up and now down you undulate.
Not given to drumming much, one has to say,
With crimson nape you brighten Winter grey;
Calling, not many list'ners you baffle,
It has earned you the nickname of Yaffle.

PILEATED WOODPECKER

Nothing quite like it, the silence can fill,
First thoughts can be "That's a pneumatic drill."
Surely few forest sounds can it eclipse,
Observe the great holes, the pile of wood chips;
So, what has done it? What's the tree wrecker?
None other than Pileated Woodpecker.
Carpenter ants are the favourite snack,
At finding these insects they have the knack,
Keen hearing informs them where the prey lurk,
Losing no time at all, they set to work,
The trunk is hammered, a large hole, oblong
Is fashioned to satisfy their penchant,
Leaving the borehole, appetite sated,
A potential dray has been created.
In mitigation, it has to be said,
Most trees chosen are unsound, if not dead.
When pounding's finished, those birds have the gall
To wake the echoes with their raucous call.

WAGTAILS

Quivering appendage, a dead giveaway,
Not long that one searches in vain,
For one of these quite small active darters,
Tail moving in vertical plane.

Motacillation, perhaps one should say,
In describing the wagging stern,
They can also call fairly loudly too,
Not usually too taciturn.

In flight recognised, rather distinctive
As they dip and jerk overmuch,
It is hardly a steady performance
They're just a bit hard on the clutch.

There's Pied everpresent throughout the year,
Likewise the Grey, handsome fellow,
Whilst the White just appears here on passage,
One can't face Winter, it's Yellow!

THE DIPPER

A waterside bird, and looking for grub,
Under water, in the Sub Aqua Club,
Still for a while, then down rocks it will tread,
Submerging and walking along the bed
Of fast flowing streams, that is the first choice,
Quite low, swift in flight, and shrill in the voice;
Midstream on a stone there standing alert,
A neat dapper Dipper in a white shirt
Proclaiming its presence, a far white blob,
And very evident curtsey or bob,
With a chestnut cummerbund in the Spring,
A delightful touch to the day you bring;
At home under water, seems odd to swash
In the shallows when enjoying a wash.

THE WREN

Troglodytes, Troglodytes,
What a mouthful, for such a mite is,
The humble farthing your print bore,
But your namesake built St Paul's, and more,
In the bushes, in low scrub
You can make a right hubbub,
That loud voice with Stentor vies,
Disproportionate to your size,
Hyperactive, little, fat,
In almost any habitat;
Tireless suitor you take no rests,
Till you have constructed several nests,
In the sure hope that one, if any
Will be accepted by your Jenny.
Aggressive posture, so much alive,
You'll adapt, and you'll survive.
Troglodyte means cave dweller of course,
But you'll also nest in heather or gorse.
Taken for granted, but nice to see,
Little brown job how we love thee.

THE FLYCATCHERS

Birds of the broad-leaved trees, one's the Spotted,
Upright the stance, as the tail often rocks,
And among the oaks, the Pieds are dotted,
In woodland theatre taking a box.

First on the scene, in Spring, there comes the Pied,
Scarce leafed the trees, so shows well that white vest,
Later, Spotted, it's easier to hide,
Needing to forage to construct a nest.

Alert on a branch with that big dark eye,
It's concentrating on the insects there,
And woe betide an unsuspecting fly
That ventures into that bird's thoroughfare.

Nature's provided that bill, bold and black,
Just the right instrument for its function,
Manageable Diptera to attack,
An insectivore without compunction.

They will subjugate those that sting and bite,
Persevering in that feeding caper,
Showing attentive deviating flight,
Lethal as suspended sticky paper.

THAT NIGHTINGALE

The songbird which, it is said, all others beats,
Which has inspired such as Coleridge and Keats,
How we hoped that it was not an idle tale,
When we got wind of a Chudleigh Knighton-gale!
So one May morning down past Bovey Tracey
We went, explored, then heard it, loud and pacy,
Unique song sustained and rendered in the day,
Or in the dark, a rich mix one has to say,
Of sweetest notes together with a jangle,
It was performed deep in a scrubby tangle;
As we closed our eyes 'twas easy to declare
That transported we had been to Berkeley Square,
But were we to see it? At the bit we chafed,
Until a cursory glimpse we were vouchsafed;
From now on, that patch is almost hallowed ground,
Where Philomel practised that emotive sound.

SONG THRUSH

How pleasurable that forceful song,
So indefatigable, livelong,
That's the Throstle, on top branches sat,
Its favourite singing habitat,
Thriving its voice on iteration,
Vocalist without relaxation;
Such vigorous communicator,
And, of the Spring, prognosticator,
Experienced snail depredator,
The latter mercilessly battered,
Shell, scant protection, so soon shattered,
And fragments willy-nilly scattered,
Gasteropod molluscs a delight,
And so surely the most relished bite,
They tickle the turdine appetite;
Most handsomely spotted on the breast,
In our gardens a most welcome guest
Strange that its namesake is an inflamed throat,
When from that bird such tones melodic float.

CHOUGHS

The Alpine ones, at sev'ral thousand feet,
Among Europe's high-tops, that is their beat,
Happy to summer up near the snow caps,
Competing with Marmots for tourist scraps,
How chuffed they are to be, one would suppose,
Among the most altitudinal Crows.
Strange that it can live in a harsher clime
Than its British cousin, who at this time,
Only in Wales can command a living;
Measures in hand, a chance it's been given,
Re-colonise Cornwall, that's the idea,
The Duchy's cliffs, again, that call should hear;
So if seen flying, noisy, athletic,
News of revival, we hope prophetic,
And may the bills red and yellow flourish,
Continue our birding zest to nourish.

THE JACKDAW

Colonial nester, consorter of Rooks,
And you've found your way into poetry books,
In Ingoldsby Legends they've found you a place,
Albeit in ecclesiastic disgrace,
Stealing that ring, the Lord Cardinal's treasure,
And earning his Eminence's displeasure.
Noisy, gregarious, so often in flocks
And you're all over black but for those grey locks,
It's not for long that you can keep your mouth shut,
And when on the ground you will walk with a strut;
Pilfering the small birds' food from the garden,
Without a by-your-leave or beg-your-pardon,
Then it's insult to injury you can add,
As it's sometimes a young Spring nestling you've had.
When it comes to nesting your choice can be wide,
Trees, cliffs, or buildings, you'll find somewhere to hide.

THE RAVEN

The largest of the Crows, with powerful stroke,
And far off it can be heard, that porcine croak,
It's not uncommon in the West,
And with that jizz one is impressed,
Of other species, not many will provoke.

Facing Flood, first from the Ark, a Raven led;
In famine, found flesh for Elijah, and bread;
'Tween Locksmith, Maypole, Rudge did slip,
But all the while he kept a "Grip",
Whilst "Nevermore", Poe's precocious Raven said.

Early in the year there's nidification,
Massive structure, daring Winter's privation,
And it's for life that they will pair,
And they will dominate the air,
With an extraordinary demonstration.

IN THE FIELD

RSPB RIVER TAMAR CRUISE — December 1987

We boarded the "Plymouth Venturer"
At Saltash, it was cold, it was wet,
But with Tony's co-operation
Some good birds we intended to get.

Varied Ducks and Gulls when we started,
Those were merely hors d'oeuvres, a prelude,
For, on the next mud bank, there they were,
Special Waders, renowned pulchritude.

Wasn't much water under the keel
Where the Avocets were to be found,
To get even closer, grandstand view,
The "Venturer" was then run aground.

Such dainty carriage, beautiful birds,
Like chorus girls graceful and nimble,
Understandable how they became
The RSPB's chosen symbol.

Sev'ral counts were made of those waders,
Something over three figures was seen,
The number finally accepted,
Avocets — one hundred and sixteen.

Into the Sound, and doing ten knots,
Fading light, some drizzle, rather dull,
A remarkably lynx-eyed watcher
Sighted Mediterranean Gull.

Back to Saltash, and into the coach,
How welcome would have been a duvet,
Albeit most of us we'd go again,
Like *Tamarrow*, I would have to say!

WEST SEDGEMOOR — January 1988

Scarce risen the sun, the sky red in the East,
The birders of Torridge don't mind in the least,
We travelled in comfort, no cramped excursion,
It worked out roughly at four seats per person,
Expecting to see many birds, wetland kind,
But when we reached Sedgemoor, then what did we find . . . ?

Chorus — Mud, Mud, laborious Mud,
Thoughts of a picnic were nipped in the bud,
In the Somerset Levels, it was the Devil's
Own job to stay upright, laborious Mud.

We soon saw some Swans, not too far, on the route,
They made not a sound, and what's more they were Mute,
However beyond them, and further afield,
Some twenty odd Bewick's to us were revealed,
We could not get too close, and our trouble's source,
Was a ten-foot wide ditch, brim full, and of course . . .

It's three hundred years, give or take two or three
Since similar barrier changed history,
Monmouth, a by-blow of King Charles the second,
Had a claim to the throne, strong, so some reckoned;
His troops down at Sedgemoor were doing quite fair,
Till they met a wide ditch, and also was there . . .

When the time came to leave, backs turned on the scene,
And bilious as budgies at what might have been,
We'd hoped that a Harrier would have been about,
Short-eared Owl, maybe Snipe, but we had dipped out,
Next time we'll be lucky, see them from the hide,
Meanwhile what's the memory that will most abide . . .

LUNDY ISLAND TRIP — May 1988
(or "Those procrastinating Puffins")

One misty morning on Bideford quay,
Met an ornithological horde,
Tickets showed departure time — half past nine,
But by then we weren't even aboard.

Lundy they call it, that's Puffin in Norse,
And out there it lies in mid-channel,
We set off to see those colourful Auks,
We now think it was so much flannel.

Early in May and book said "Never fear,
All the Auks will be back, yes indeed."
What was not mentioned, not on any page,
Was that Puffins have not learnt to read.

Two hundred and fifty odd of us went,
Most were crowded on Oldenburg's deck,
Anyone see a Puffin on Lundy?
And the answer is No, did they heck.

Now disembarking can take quite a time,
One tender, twenty people can fill,
Once ashore, puffin' was heard, though not seen,
As some climbed that precipitous hill.

The weather stayed fair, sun even appeared,
And it surely exceeded our hopes,
You could say that there was just one shower,
That was us with our bins and our 'scopes.

But sure we'll see Puffins on the West side,
Circumnavigating soon OK,
But one would have needed eye of an 'awk!
We were rocking a bit far away.

Having said all that, there were a few folk,
Who declared they had been face to face,
There on the shelf in the Tavern of course,
Puffin stuffed, and it's in a glass case.

However don't think that we were browned off,
Because those Puffins chose to frustrate,
I'm sure that we all enjoyed it, and got
Sev'ral ticks for nineteen-eighty-eight.

HORNER WOOD — May 1988

Exmoor in Spring was a prospect to please,
As it transpired we were glad of the trees;
We met at Exford, then drove on the moor,
It was blowing hard, it began to pour,
The six of us donned our all weather gear,
And descended a grassy bank quite sheer,
Sure-footed we all got safely below,
Horner Wood then sheltered us from the blow;
We followed a track beside a swift stream,
In showers short, occasional sun's gleam,
Then wading and crossing from bank to bank,
The unleaved oak and beech we had to thank
For revealing migrants, put in good heart
By getting Pied Flycatcher and Redstart,
The smart male birds were such a joy to see,
As they perched, then flitted from tree to tree;
Warblers, the Chiffchaff, the Willow, the Wood
Nesting, preoccupied with parenthood.
Grey Wagtail and Dipper skimming the burn,
Then disappearing mid boulder and fern.
Additional, worthy of mention too
Were Green Woodpecker, Buzzard and Cuckoo.
Up through the wood, we watched them infiltrate,
A Red Deer herd, we counted twenty-eight.
So Horner had fulfilled each prediction,
With regret we made our valediction.

CHAPEL WOOD — May 1988
(or "Open the box")

Oh we went down to the wood one day,
There was Cyril set to please,
As Warden, he was ensuring that
We saw the wood for the trees,
Of arboriculture he did tell,
Where to plant, and when to fell,
And check the boxes, are there any tenants?

Big Dave climbed up to a likely box,
The tree, and the ladder shook,
Poor little Tits were certainly Blue,
He lifted their roof to look,
A nearby Flycatcher, it's a Pied,
Handsome male's identified,
And he's the occupant of number twenty.

Indulging our hobby, we saw one,
Flying just over the wood,
That will be bird of the day for us,
And that resolution stood,
This Falcon so fast on sickle wing,
A Swift will be suffering,
When being hunted hard, for hungry *Hobblets*.

There are big black birds that have their pad,
At the top of highest pine,
Looks hardly safe, are they raven mad?
Those dark characters corvine,
They don't use bricks, just bundles of sticks,
Hard luck if the wind plays tricks,
Somehow, though croaking, they survive the weather.

LYNMOUTH — June 1988
(or "Nice one Cyril")

'Twas a June evening when "October Morning"
Went astern from the Lynmouth beach,
With a party of North Devon birders,
And with Cyril along to teach.

We chugged ever westward, surveying the cliffs,
For nesting Gulls, Auks and the like,
We were watching, and listening expectant,
For Cyril was "manning" the mike.

There were so many Auks on those ledges, high,
As well that they keep very still,
Were they looking at us, showing interest,
Did those Guillemots "raise a bill"?

The evening sun shone on those dense-packed faces,
Visibility good, and yet,
We could not be sure if those Razorbills,
Were Wilkinson, Bic, or Gillette!

The solicitous Auks arriving with food,
At fishing they know the angles!
When regurgitating stuff to their young,
It looks to have been through mangles.

So thanks to the skipper, and to Cyril, of course,
For his most informative talk,
And showing us all those dwellings high rise,
Which gladly we'll leave to the Auk.

THE SKERN/KENWITH — August 1988
(or "Bins to the Dump")

We met at Northam, party quite large,
It was raining, and rather grey,
But with the Okehampton company
We were soon enjoying the day,
Inter-group fraternisation's fine,
When out on an expedition,
As we suffer each other's puns and
Criticise soundness of vision.

We all met down at the coast again,
And there was a lot to *diSKERN*,
See the Gulls in the sky, how they twist,
And also watch that Sandwich Tern!
Some had a Calidris Canutus,
And they're quite sure that's what they got,
That's until somebody confused them,
By saying "Oh yes it is Knot!"

We're attracted to the Rubbish Dump,
We dislike the smell and the waste,
But there was an Iceland Gull present,
And there's no accounting for taste,
Picturesque? The area's nice if
You like Power Stations besides
The above-mentioned tip and shipyards,
And acres of mud at low tides.

There were a great number of Waders,
Most near to the edge of the tide,
And some could scarcely be seen at all,
Among rocks and seaweed they hide,
Does one spend a long motionless watch,
And in the same place does one stay,
Or does one make short return visits,
Sort of ''Little Stints'' one might say.

Later on a travel to Kenwith,
The topic of conversation,
Was only a Ring-necked Duck no less,
There in urban preservation,
It's so surprising what can appear,
In this tiny Bideford patch,
There have been unusual callers,
That more famous sites cannot match.

TAMAR LAKES — December 1988
(or "Out for a Duck")

Half in Cornwall, Half in Devon,
Tamar Lakes, can be bird heaven,
We had species forty-seven,
That December day.

Grab the fence, don't throw your hand in,
All that mud, it's so demanding,
Should you fall it's notwithstanding!
Try and keep your feet.

Upper Lake where many duck float,
Long-tailed's best, that must be our vote,
Pity we can't go back by boat,
And avoid the mire.

Flashing from the reed-beds, we see
Small brown jobs, what are they? Surely
With that *lift*-off, *Jack* Snipe, must be!
Are they jet-propelled?

Gadwall, Goldeneye, Gold Plovers,
Shoveler, Pochard, Teal from covers,
Peregrine for all bird lovers,
These and many more.

Song Thrush, Stonechat, Meadow Pipit,
Bullfinch, Reed Bunting, and Peewit,
Buzzard, Kingfisher, and Bluetit,
'Mongst the Passerines.

There's no doubt that we'll take good care,
See those lakes again, a great pair,
Something must be in the air there,
On the water too.

SLAPTON — September 1989
(or "Reed all about it!")

The North Devon Party to South Devon came,
We were lucky, the weather was dry;
Some said we would see Little Gull and Black Tern,
But that proved to be a Slapton Ley!

We were dropped at the door of the hide, just right,
We sat there, and, it to say, suffice,
In the reeds and the scrub, the Warblers appeared,
Just like that, straight away, in a trice.

Some people got Cetti's, also Reed and Sedge,
With a Whitethroat and Willow, but stay,
A most favoured few, they saw an Aquatic,
Water find! It was bird of the day.

As we watched out to sea, the cupboard was bare,
Notwithstanding we were soon to learn,
That that not too very inviting outlook,
Could do for us many a good Tern!

The Terns they were Common and Sandwich, as well,
With the Ley also part of their patch,
In spite of that they were still rather wary,
For they knew that in there was a catch!

Staring to seaward where sharp eyes are needed,
To pick up the fliers and floaters,
Why do some of them, in the waves, sink so low,
As those so very Common Scoters!

Now if waterfowl to you are confusing,
And you can't pick one out of the ruck,
And if you're right out of practice, and rusty,
Why so were those Ferruginous Duck!

Contented we were at the end of the day,
As we all climbed back into the bus,
For, with a Sparrowhawk, and a few Waders,
Species total was some forty plus.

DAWLISH WARREN/POWDERHAM — November 1989
(or "Exe marks the spot")

We were promised rain, but we didn't care,
We expected a good haul of birds down there.
In the event we were granted a boon,
It didn't turn wet until late afternoon.
With bins alert, by that time we had seen
Quite a number of species, land and marine;
We had trudged the sands of Dawlish Warren
An ornithological Legion Foreign.
At Powderham Park the Fallow Deer herds
Were in marked contrast to the absence of birds,
But once on the wall, beside the river,
Then rose expectations, hearts were a-quiver,
Recurvirostra Avosetta
Was the promised appetite whetter;
Walked to the Turf, that should have paid us,
We'd see Avocets, dainty waders,
But sad to tell there were just none,
One hundred plus? There was not one.
Yet a very good birding day, ye wist,
As you will see from the separate list.

HARTLAND POINT/TAMAR LAKES — December 1989

(The coast was wild, but the Lakes were Tamar)

A cold but dry morning at Hartland,
Where we parked; without moving a pace
We stood there admiring that Raptor,
With a pleased Peregrine on each face!

Now here's a curious confusion,
"Red-throated" declared every member,
Referring to sev'ral nice Divers,
But they have White Throats in December.

Sea-birds will hunt far for their family,
They catch wet fish, of course, plenty too,
Some young can consume thirty kilos,
Ere leaving the nest! Gannet be true?

Tamar Lakes, p.m. destination,
And the expectancy you could feel,
And though we saw Goldeneye, Pochard,
We'd been Wigeon for that Blue-winged Teal.

Lower Lake, the place where we ended
The day, with the light in fast decline,
Did somebody see a Crake or Rail?
Or could he have been shooting a line?

Once again Okehampton and Torridge
Joined forces, on a day set to please,
As usual we had equal measure
Of wry humour and straight expertise.

CHEW VALLEY LAKE — February 1990
(or "Watchers in seventh Avon!")

As we moved the showers threatened,
Soon enough the morn grew wetter,
But we're birding o'er the Mendips,
To that Lake, you can't Chews better!

Once arrived the rain relented,
Though light was poor, and wind force six,
Never mind, we were delighted,
As we clocked up more annual ticks.

Waterfowl in great profusion,
Yes, we were certainly in luck,
Blooming Coot, confounded Moorhen,
Also a host of Ruddy Duck!

All three Sawbills too were present,
And gradually they came in view,
First Goosander, then Merganser,
Later the Avon Ladies . . . . . . Smew.

We don't hesitate to mention,
In fact indeed we do request,
Birders should go down to Chew, there's
Such a lot for you to digest!

POWDERHAM/TURF/EXMINSTER — March 1990
(or "Was Avocet a tick in the mud!")

Ideal *Habitat*, open all week,
With good stock of what we'd come to seek,
Such a fine selection on display,
And a treat in store there was that day.

There were water birds, all kinds galore,
As we scanned across from shore to shore,
You're never quite sure what you will see,
For Exe is the unknown quantity.

Oh the Exe is broad, the Exe is wide,
It's a long way to the other side;
When distantly a duck you espy,
It will be a common Goldeneye.

A Common Goldeneye, nothing more,
And all other versions we deplore,
With other ideas we mustn't toy,
That drake, it was not a Barrow(s) Boy!

Waders plenty, no need to look hard,
Including Godwit, both Black and Barred,
Those Grey Plover in their breeding jet,
And overt avian Avocet,

They're cashing in, and they are not slow,
It's only open when tide is low,
Making withdrawals from the Mud Bank,
There are Oystercatchers and Redshank.

Warblers, and Warblers, and some can sing,
They're delightful harbingers of Spring,
But one with raucous call, we met is,
A skulking loud-mouthed type called Cetti's.

So many sorts of aquatic bird,
Seen on the river, the thought occurred,
Though varied sizes with varied marks,
They're all one species, they're just MUD-LARKS.

YARNER WOOD — May 1990

Watching the Taw before we set off,
When some hopes were excitedly built,
In the haze, a long-legged wader,
Could have been yet one more Black-winged Stilt.

Alas such ideas were soon cancelled,
Younger eyes scanned along the mud bank,
The decision was made quite quickly,
"That bird there is a common Greenshank."

A hot day it was, down at Yarner,
We were glad of some shade, and yet still,
The Wood Warblers did not feel the heat,
As they "shivered", deliv'ring their trill.

Pied Flycatchers there were in plenty,
They'd no need to look far for a bunk,
Unlike some other woodland species,
They much prefer a box to a trunk!

Some of us kept quite a long vigil,
Watching a hole in a tree stump tall,
Woodpecker was not Lesser Spotted,
It was not even spotted at all!

The hole in that stump we were assured,
Was made by that tiny Woodpecker,
But later we were rather doubtful,
And thought it was by Black and Decker.

Now take someone new to the pastime,
To Yarner midst the trees and the plants,
They'll be bitten by the birding bug,
Or maybe by those teeming Wood Ants.

PRAWLE POINT — May 1990
(or "Have a flag day, find that Bunting!")

There's a resident bird though it's rare,
Now confined to those few miles square,
So it's just the place to go hunting,
The Prize, that elusive Cirl Bunting.

Prawle Point was the southern location,
The end of our peregrination,
There it sang with not too much clamour,
Like a forgetful Yellowhammer.

Someone with us is watching the sea,
Telling us there's a bird he can see,
But the ref'rence point gives little joy,
If one can't see that flaming red buoy!

A haze rather limited vision,
Made it hard to reach a decision,
Was that a Razorbill? Guillemot?
Or was it like an Auk? Not a lot.

But closer in, each one a viewer,
We thought it meet, we got a Skua.
Steady low flight, it was going west,
Like poor chicks will from some sea-birds' nest.

Proceeding along Pig's Nose Valley,
Need good migrants to swell our tally,
No unusual visitors about,
You could say "At Pig's Nose there was s . . . nowt!"

We've all heard those remarks, without fail,
That almost inevitable tale,
"Not much about as far as I know,
You should have been here two weeks ago!"

Thus the Warden, who observes and records,
Whose work on that hillside one applauds,
We trust the migrants notice will pay,
That the slope will incline them to stay.

RSPB RIVER EXE TRIP — December 1990

An RSPB river cruise,
No need the merits to effuse,
What better than the Exe to choose,
For some winter birding.

At Exmouth there we went aboard,
So many but with one accord,
All those water birds to record,
General ambition.

"Devon Princess" anchors aweigh,
First took us out into the bay,
The sev'ral sea fowl to survey,
Grebe, Eider, Merganser.

The tide, now flooding well upstream,
We turned to where the waders teem,
With Exmouth on the starboard beam,
We travelled up river.

True aficionados who'll
See such concentration and drool,
Will keep eyes on sandbank and pool,
Can't afford to dip out.

We knew there would be, on parade,
Large numbers of those birds that wade,
Avocets have the accolade,
They always winter there.

Oystercatchers, Golden Plover,
Knot, both Godwits, we discover,
Avocet and Shanks, Oh Brother,
There are so many more.

Grey Plover, Curlew, Sanderling,
There's Dunlin, Turnstone and Lapwing,
Threatening all came Peregrine,
It's hungrily twitching.

On the trip we were kept au fait,
The bridge's info, prompt relay,
A constant bird communiqué,
Spoon-fed aviculture.

The day, it was a great success,
Fifty plus species did impress,
A royal time with the ''Princess'',
Exe-cellent birding ground.

THE "NEW" ROADFORD RESERVOIR — January 1991

The old firm of Torridge/Okehampton,
Paid their first combined visit down there,
The perimeter tracks we tramped on,
Possibilities? We were aware.

Twenty odd of us curious souls,
For birders will it be academe?
And become one of those twitchers' goals,
Though it's not all that long been on stream.

The rain continued to dog our trip,
But by no means was thc cupboard bare,
Though nothing to, up a frenzy, whip
It was for sure, more than meagre fare.

There were bread and butter birds enough,
On it could we hopefully have jam,
But if a Smew had been in to loaf!
Then into our Ken it had not swam!

Grebe, Wigeon, Teal, Pochard, Goldeneye,
The ubiquitous Mallard and Coot,
Redwing, Fieldfare, Treecreeper, Magpie,
And more ere we ended our pursuit.

Activity was curtailed at lunch,
Through continuous, incessant rain,
There was strong feeling, more than a hunch,
That we would be down that way again.

That lake should answer problems of drought,
And Ranger Ken will the site enhance,
Whilst running water won't be in doubt,
And idling birds get a Spalding chance!

DORSET DISCOVERY — April 1991

If it's birds you're after, you should hobnob,
In Hardy country with Jamie and Bob;
"The Dorset Naturalist", they provide
Facilities second to none, you'll ride,
In a Transit minibus, comfy, serene,
And you'll cover the distances between,
Ornithologically friendly sites,
With each one offering its own delights.
When memories of breakfast get remote,
It will be time for Jamie's cuisine haute,
Imaginative packed lunch, it's a boon,
Will sustain you right through the afternoon,
That Spring weekend, for birds, we did so well,
With one hundred and more there were to tell.
Warblers at Radipole serenading,
Some varied Terns, and Calidrids wading,
At Ferry Bridge nearby, along the shore,
Then off we went to Portland Bill for more,
Here came the sea-birds flying eastward fast,
Some Gannets, and Shags and Scoters, all passed,
The Kittiwakes from the cliff were calling
What's going to stop those Auks from falling,
So precariously perched on edges,
With such vertiginous views from ledges.
Swallows, and Martins too, were arriving,
And inland, the Passerines were thriving,
To Langton Herring, we went, on the Fleet,
And what should be there for us, quite a treat,
Some Bar-tailed Godwit, mainly summer hued,
And piscivorous Sandwich Terns we viewed.
A fox came trotting, and its jaws were closed,
Around its prey, a rat, and we supposed,
The cubs would be eating a rodent course
At their vulpine villa beneath the gorse.
And now, across the Fleet, the Cuckoo's come,
That most unwelcome visitor for some.

Durlston Head next day where the cliff-top scrub,
Rang to a happy avian hubbub,
With Tits, Warblers, and Pipits, might and main,
So gladly celebrating Spring again;
Pleasant morning, we were never gladder,
Only snake in the grass, was an Adder!
Myopic Woodpecker, it sought a bole,
But it made do with a telegraph pole,
On then to Arne where we studied the board,
Reading there what birds we hoped to record,
And for a bonus, we'd a splendid sight,
It was a Spotted Redshank black as night,
The same as the tails of the Godwits here,
Such elegant birds they always appear.
To the final venue, the heath named Gore,
And the local special was what we saw,
The Dartford Warbler did itself present,
Though a long way from the county of Kent;
Then, to round off so well the final day,
A Hobby came, chasing its flying prey.

TO LUNDY WITH OUR GORDON ISLANDER — June 1991

It was the good ship Oldenburg,
That sailed from Torridge quay,
Full complement of passengers,
Rare birds we hoped to see.

The Devon Birders chartered it,
As was their wont each year,
For a Lundy day excursion,
"Dip out" we wouldn't hear.

That Auk we knew was back again
And some were out to get
A lifer, crippler, mega tick,
That Ancient Murrelet.

So far adrift, so well off course,
It's flown an ocean wide,
'Twas said it courted Razorbill
When looking for a bride.

The steep ascent once climbed, we pierced
The murk for Jenny's Cove,
Though wanting visibility,
Into dim view it hove.

And the wet mist it rolled in low
And the wet mist it rolled in thick,
And scarcely could we see two yards,
As parrots we were sick.

In course of time we were vouchsafed
Clear view, and we did gawk,
Found were its avian cousins,
Not the Alaskan Auk.

At Millcombe there had been for days,
They said, a Woodchat Shrike,
Its absence was conspicuous,
Who'd told it "On yer bike?"

The island highland dropped astern,
We had a slight regret,
We shall another visit pay,
But will that Murrelet?

PORTLAND AND RADIPOLE — September 1991
(or ''Weymouth go down there to see again'')

Our first destination Portland, looking closely at the sea,
It's a splendid place for spotting, as all birders will agree,
For the Spring and Autumn migrants, there are some for
  which you'd kill,
And there's something seems to call you, ''Come you back to
  watch the Bill''.

It was bright but it was breezy, and the Channel boiled with
  foam,
Not too many birds were flying as the waves we tried to comb,
Came a big one, see him twisting, turning now, and what's
  more he's
Got a Shearwater's credentials, it was one known as Cory's.

So improbably but truly, came a ''Condor'' through the spray,
Bearing passengers from Jersey, let me hasten then to say.
The long-necked Cranes were resident, hoisting stone not
  taking wing,
Whilst a Kite aloft and flying was controlled up there by string.

Next we travelled on to Weymouth for that special urban goal,
Quite a spacious lake and reed-beds, yes you know, it's
  Radipole,
Here some of the breeding species didn't fail, they showed up
  good
And that Sandpiper, no carving, though it's classified as Wood.

There can be a varied Gull choice, there'll be Med ones in the
  troop,
And in the accepted Order they are first in their own Group,
So Top Laridae can be At Radipole, a statement plain,
In addition it's an anagram, as you will ascertain.

A great day we had in Dorset, and of that there is no doubt,
You may not always get your ''prey'', but the quarry will
  stand out;
There's so much room for migrants, and the sea-birds have
  sheer water,
Observation is superb, you can see from every quarter.

SLIMBRIDGE — December 1991

Oh to be in Slimbridge, now that Winter's there,
And whoever goes to Slimbridge sees so many fowls in care
With the geese arriving in thousands, Great Scott,
Sir Peter ensured none went to pot,
While the stately Bewick's take a bow,
In Slimbridge now.

It was Stormin' Norman who took the wheel,
And the hearts of the Pheasants sank,
We said goodbye, and spirits were high,
Though not in the petrol tank.

Through the mist and the fog we cruised so well,
There were fifteen of us aboard,
We gave three cheers, and we had five gears,
Us in Transit, in a Ford!

We arrived and parked, at the Wildfowl Trust,
With bins and 'scopes at the ready,
We're moving quick, not to miss a tick,
The total's mounting steady.

There were bright colours in some of the Fowl,
The Mandarin, and Wood Duck shone,
In contrast to, some of pallid hue,
Snow Geese pale, and Bewick's wan!

From South Finger hides, at the extreme north,
We saw a sleepy-looking bird,
For its pillow a pollard willow,
Little Owl couldn't be heard!

Only one saw that Ring-necked Parakeet,
The others queried his vision,
And they inferred, you could use that word,
It surely lacked precision!

Amongst the thousands of White-fronted Geese,
'Twas said one was the Lesser breed,
We went cross-eyed, it was never spied,
It follows, didn't succeed!

We all decided, it's been a great day,
So close to the River Severn,
We didn't smile when we checked the dial,
Will it get us to Dev'n?

CORNISH COAST — February 1992
(or "To Hayle and back")

The dawn broke anything but fine,
After quick snatch of tea and toast,
We're soon on the A39,
And it's on birds we have design,
Down to the Cornish Coast.

Baker's dozen of us unwind,
Not too much room for knees and toes,
This time we had a bird in mind
At Stratton, there we hoped to find
This one at Speedwell Close.

So at that Close began our quest,
Hoping to find that brown job rare,
Identifying was a test,
But flags wave for the Bunting guest,
Away we ourselves tear.

We go then into Cornwall deep,
Greeted with Hayle! Whose birds so well
Enjoy the estuary mud heap,
Uneasy Egret with first peep
We got, then Hayle farewell!

On to St Ives to scour the sea
Where estimable creatures pass,
We were rewarded handsomely,
Those Dolphins though proved not to be
A school, but a small class!

Black-throated Diver in the bay,
Also Med Gull, then pulses stir,
For that small bird, bird of the day,
A Little Auk, that's not to say
Cockney Accipiter!

Again the Egret did we find,
Ring-billed Gull was also resting,
In that Creek, just a bit confined,
An area bit unrefined,
Copper-house not arresting!

Called at the Moor but nothing showed,
No Harriers Bursdon the scene!
A special day, as back we rode,
We trust no one got Pigeon-toed,
And for the next we're keen.

MINIBUS — PORTLAND, LODMOOR, RADIPOLE — May 1992

Off again, we're making for Dorset,
Spring arrivals, that's what we've in mind,
Now Norman was good, there weren't any
Of those too close encounters, bird kind.

So making good time to Ferry Bridge,
That's where we had our first birding stop,
And there those delightful Little Terns,
Of our bill had to be the most top.

Then on to Portland, pleasant and warm,
And where many twitchers had been lured,
To look for that mega rarity,
Little Lark so closely pedicured!

Short-toed Lark was missing, but migrants,
Were making themselves known all around,
Our hearts leapt at the constant birdsong,
And Linnets and Warblers did abound.

Roseate Tern, they said, at Lodmoor,
There were all of us straining our necks,
But the only way to have found it
Would have been through some rose-coloured specs!

To Radipole, there to be greeted
By explosive calls, you can bet he's
That little brown Warbler, not too shy
Soon showing, yes, one of those Cetti's,

There also a nice drake Goldeneye,
Solitary and ever so near,
Putting on a brave courting display,
Alas, no duck was seen to appear.

Another, for most, too, was missing,
Special Tit of the marsh and the fen,
"Ping" was not heard, no Reedling was seen,
So, unBearded, they stayed in their den!

Once more we had a very good day,
With some seventy plus as the score,
The district, we always en-Dorset!
We could not have expected Lodmoor!

MINIBUS — NORTH DORSET/HAMPSHIRE — June 1992
(or "Good spotting . . . . . Nissan persons found!")

The Minibus took us east again, and we were trav'lling grandly,
Until doubts were strongly felt, like, "Have they moved
Sixpenny Handley?"
Ah yes, that cut-price village, we were missing it, you know,
And the navigation error, it was blamed on so-and-so,
The bloke that they dubbed "Pedro", under a straw sombrero.

But arrived where we'd intended; without much searching
and hunting,
We got, *amaizingly* enough, a cacophonous *Corn* Bunting!
Somewhat later, having opted to move to some fresh ground,
There came that special Harrier, of that Colonel's name
renowned,
So after moving round, the superb Montagu's was found.

Now this fine male Harrier did not appear to be true to type,
Had he been cashiered in disgrace, and had he relinquished
his stripe?
This superior Raptor, as illustrated in books,
He has those diagnostic wing bars, for which, of course, one
looks;
He's quart'ring crannies and nooks, hoping to grab with his
hooks.

Next we watched various Lepidoptera up on Martin Down,
Quite naturally it was Adonis Blue that won the beauty crown,
Poor Fritillary, with envy, it really was Dark Green!
Dingy Skipper, in that company, was but a sad has-been;
For birds again we were keen, then stout patellas were seen.

Over there were the breeding Thick-Knees, alias Stone
Curlew pair,
They are birds with a strange expression, giving us a baleful
stare.
Would you have a beaming smile and utterly delight us
If in those swollen joints you had immutable arthritis?
Intriguing species, quite a plus, certainly worth a fuss.

Having enjoyed so much ornithological satisfaction,
Now a long cold drink was fast becoming an added attraction,
At the Coote Arms in Martin, there we subsequently braked,
And with a cooling draught our near insatiable thirst we slaked,
The local news wasn't faked, three Grey Partridges were waked.

Then back through Dorset easily we came, no failure, no
mishap,
No second opinion necessary, no reference to a map,
In Somerset we stopped to pay a visit to Sedgemoor,
Inappeasable us birders, always adding to the score,
The light by now was poor, but Little Owl, the mouse it saw.

MINIBUS — DORSET SPRING — April 1993
(or ''Make mine a migrant'')

The Torridge Eleven set off in the bus,
They have a fixture in Dorset, to meet,
There are some good grounds, and popular pitches,
Portland, Lodmoor, Radipole, and the Fleet.

First destination that peninsula bleak,
It was blowing uncomfortably chill,
But there it was appropriately enough,
Down at Portland where we met up with Bill.

As up and down Channel the sea-birds they went,
Scoter and Shearwater there were to greet,
And were those Auks on the watch for 'edge Sparrows.
Or those Arctic Skuas stabbing cold meat?

Contrastingly watching white water, black birds,
With our tick tally soon getting riper,
And not surprising, it was rather frigid,
How very Purple was that Sandpiper.

Came the moment to bid farewell to Portland,
When Time's chariot, for us, had fast winged,
The next stop Ferry Bridge, did not see mist nets,
But those fat Plovers were certainly Ringed!

So to Lodmoor, there's a Little Ringed Plover,
That's what we're told, will it stay for our sake?
It saw us coming, but we went one better,
With a most obliging Garganey drake.

This super dabbler had everyone drooling,
Some had scarce ever before looked upon,
It was, most convincingly, Bird of the Day,
And that was easily carried, Nem Con.

To Radipole, where the ''Wind in the Willows''
And reed-beds, meant few birds openly sang,
The Sedge Warblers and Cetti's made themselves heard,
But there was no sign of Ken Grahame's gang!

MINIBUS — HALDON, AYLESBURY, WOODBURY — July 1993

Unrelenting, the rain as we motored,
The Minibus party once more,
Bill took us along that tortuous road,
No trouble this time with the door.

Almost deserted, so dismal Haldon,
As up to the viewpoint we steered,
Every bird proved to be a Woodpigeon,
That's until that Honey appeared.

Obliging, it perched on a tall dead stump,
Just resting, or looking for bees?
Then a flat-winged performance preceded
Departure behind the pine trees.

Woodbury Castle, our thoughts turned to Hobby,
Such an ideal habitat, prime,
But no sightings had we of that Falcon,
For a Hobby was it past time?

Aylesbeare Common amidst gorse and bracken,
Dartford Warblers, active were found,
Looking after a very young family,
Distributing square meals around.

As the light failed we waited for Nightjar,
At half-nine the first did occur,
We were pleased it was not any later,
And greeted it with a ''What Churr''.

As to species, we got not too many,
Not a day to call ''Letter red'',
Though it's not numbers alone that counts, but,
Quality when Haldon and said.

CORNWALL — September 1993 — More Minibus Miles

Into deepest Cornish lane,
Into princely held domain,
Finding Stithian's reservoir, a large expanse,
The watery vegetation
Quite upset our expectation;
To find that transatlantic Grebe, there was no chance,
So we never spied the Pied,
All our efforts were denied,
What's more the Spotted Sand's unseen to boot,
Just missing an Osprey,
Could be that sort of day,
After all a Buzzard is no substitute.

Emphasising our bad luck,
Starter motor it got stuck,
But nearly everybody got behind to shove;
Then we set off on to Hayle
Hoping that the jinx would fail,
And it surely did, we had manna from above,
First your actual Osprey showed,
And the ranks of watchers crowed,
But panic 'mongst the water birds it spread,
Fish-eater, don't they know?
They bade it "Cheerio",
Must have looked a menace though, it must be said.

As for waders, such wade choice,
But most birders, with one voice,
Would declare that Temminck's Stint to be the winner,
Now its chances they were thin
'Gainst that hungry Peregrine,
Which we hoped would look beyond it for its dinner;
And all birds they did vamoose,
As all Hayle it was let loose.
So far we thought we had done rather well,
St Ives? Perhaps we should,
Sea prospects were not good,
So we turned back, and it was Hayle and farewell!

Round to Copperhouse, Carnsew,
But the Ring-billed didn't show,
Most probably because the spring tide topped the bank,
But Rock-pipit on boat's stern,
And two juvenile Black Tern,
And also Common ones, we didn't draw a blank,
Then we looked at Davidstow,
Was there something? Answer "No":
But at Maer Lake we got elated,
A Sandpiper was there,
'Twas said it could be rare,
And so it proved, no less, Semi-palmated.

Once again it was a day
To remember and let's say,
We can hardly wait until there is another,
Surely at the very worst,
Everybody got one "first",
And we'd always hoped a crippler we'd discover;
Ride in comfort, nomadic,
With our forays sporadic,
Whilst someone, on the road, must keep an eye,
And Cornwall did us proud,
We didn't mind the crowd
At Hayle, they all kept us in the know, forbye.

VELATOR — November 1993
(or "We dig the Burrows . . . . sometimes!")

Velator was the location,
There was no need to get upset,
Until wc climbed the bank, and poked,
Our heads above the parapet.

Across the Burrows screamed the wind,
Upon the dyke it had a grasp,
And as it checked our falt'ring way,
In Indian file, we felt the rasp!

However it was possible,
Vertical almost to remain,
But progress might have easier been,
With walking stick beside the Caen!

Predictably vain the morning,
Not too many birds to be seen,
Just as we thought of hot coffee,
Somebody told us "There's a Bean!"

We drove the toll road expectant,
There in a field was a gaggle,
White-fronted, yes, not one's a Bean,
Broad agreement, not much haggle.

Nevertheless a week later,
A flier could not navigate,
And landed there in the Burrows,
A very bold White Egret, Great.

Such a winter overshoot from the east,
Must surely be one of the mega twitches,
With its two tone legs and threatening bill,
Depleting amphibia in the ditches.

DAWLISH — November 1993
(or "Rabbit progress to the Warren!")

Now the morning was dry, overcast, cool,
As we the Minibus boarded,
And we set our course towards the south coast,
Quite sure that we'd be rewarded.

Many of us like birding at Dawlish,
Not always to go for a twitch,
But the mixture there for which we've a yen,
And those ticks can give us an itch!

To identify birds, it's a teaser
Sometimes, it's been known to perplex,
Though not a mathematical problem,
We soon found the value of Exe!

Our arrival was timed with High Water,
With room in the hide for us lot,
There we 'scoped through the masses of waders,
Some were Godwit, and some were Knot!

There was limited space for the hundreds,
Those birds of the waterside branch,
As huge flocks of shore-birds swirled, then dropped in,
An *avifaunal* avalanche.

Langstone Rock, it was our next objective,
Some needlessly puffed to the top,
Razorbill, Scoter, and Eider were seen,
With the Slavs, to meet in the chop!

So we then turned our noses to Powderham!
And there was diminishing light,
"Will we make out Avocet?" Someone said,
"I've a set idea that we might!"

The light just held, and we found Avocet,
Next, Owl prowl suggested nearby,
So off we went then to Exminster Marsh,
But Short-eared was in short supply.

Yet our hopes, overall, were lived up to,
A most satisfactory day,
'Twould certainly be no trouble to make
Each of us an habitué.

MINIBUS MEMORIES — 1991-1993

It was a Nissan Minibus
That roamed the country free,
And out on birding quests were they
That goodly company.

Some birds appear in the wrong place,
Stone Curlew, they must roam,
They shouldn't be on Martin Down,
Portland should be their home!

Now those Stone Curlew in Hampshire,
In camouflage, they drown,
My question is "Are the young ones
Covered in Martin Down?"

Sedgemoor not found too productive,
Bewick's, not much else to tell,
Though Herons are quite delighted,
For that Wood suits them Swell!

That Common's special, no question,
Dartford Warblers winging,
And specially in the Spring,
When m . . ayles be a'singing!

An airfield very extensive,
Birds can get lost, you know,
One day we'll score, so don't point a
Finger at Davidstow!

One bloke sat in a Slimbridge hide,
Whence all but he had fled,
He, only, saw the Parakeet,
The others wished him dead.

A place for waterfowl at Bude,
Where your joy can be so full,
And since there came Tony Soper,
It has even Maer pull!

Of all the bird sites where we've been,
Which will us over, bowl?
Come top of the list, get most votes,
In a snap Radipole?

At Haldon there, at Haldon there,
No geese, but slowly, high and rare
Hands of a clock you cannot see,
But Honey they will guarantee.

Near things we've had on the Link Road,
With those birds a bit too game,
Play "CHICKEN" they do, these Pheasants,
Get run over is the aim.

CHEW VALLEY LAKE/CHEDDAR RESERVOIR — January 1994 (or "An Avon for Waterfowl!")

Once more a wet start we deplore,
But we remembered days of yore,
Soon the rain stopped as heretofore,
And Mendips rose in welcome.

Herriot's Bridge where we first brake,
Our earliest sightings there we make,
Distinguishing the duck from drake,
Of several varied species.

Some dived, some dabbled, others slept,
Again some from the water leapt,
Whilst from our viewpoint, eyes windswept,
We blearily defined them.

"To Villice Bay" they said "You go,
That's where the Smew did earlier show,"
Redheads behaving like Yo-Yo,
Eventually we found them.

Goosander, Smew, some got the third,
As o'er the lake Merganser whirred,
So the three Sawbills had occurred
That magnificent trio.

At Cheddar, cold and feeling cheesed,
Until that offering made us pleased,
At which it was not to be sneezed,
That so tasty Birthday cake.

Fifty species were recorded,
And the one we most applauded,
By which we were most rewarded,
Had to be those Redhead Smew.

SLIMBRIDGE — February 1994

The Bideford contingent got to the meet,
They sort of made it fairly plain,
Barn Owl they'd seen, just so casually mentioned,
In passing, again and again!

A cold reception we had, it was snowing,
But most hides had room, cheek by jowl,
Not too many small birds at all, roundabout,
But we got fair views of the fowl!

Doyenne of the Bewick's, again there this year,
For the twenty-third time, no doubt,
That's Casino, a Pen writing history;
There next year? You can't roulette out!

A potential hazard arrived, for the fowl,
When a fox, the scene, came upon,
Were White-fronted whiter? Or Bean a runner?
Or did it make the Bewick's wan?

Perhaps surprising to find those Flamingos
Outside, surely the cold they dread,
They certainly seemed to be shivering, or,
Resignedly shaking the head.

And so passed another good Minibus day,
One last time our bins we adjust,
We're quite sure we shall go back there once again,
So The Wildfowl and Wetlands Trust!

ROADFORD RESERVOIR — February 1994

That happy combination of Okehampton and Torridge,
Met down at Roadford Reservoir on a birding forage,
There were twenty-nine souls that assembled all told,
And at the end where we gathered, it was *dam* cold.

Early on there was excitement, could it be a foretaste?
A large Raptor broke some woodland, and how our pulses raced,
And those who saw it longest, it up, they did chalk,
As Accipiter Gentilis, you know . . . . . . Goshawk.

Gordon the gen'ral took us along sodden paths and trails,
Where the trees afforded some shelter from the chilling gales,
Empty boughs, there must be plenty on the water,
But what we saw was a fraction in that quarter.

Down the lane, by Toft Farm, of the day, our last excursion,
Some in car were in the van, we envied their assertion,
That a Barn Owl they had seen; it did re-appear,
To the delight of all, for some, first of the year.

Canada, Greylag, and Snow Goose, sev'ral duck species too,
How we would have prized the one we missed, the unrivalled
Smew,
Dismewed, but not dismayed, we'd had good company,
We know well that to seek is not always to see.

PRAWLE POINT/SLAPTON — April 1994

The Southern coast, we thought well worth a call,
By Minibus, this time we went to Prawle,
And very soon we found the local pearl,
That special Bunting, a rare species, Cirl.

Out to sea, showing, Cormorant and Shag,
Gannet and Scoter added to the bag,
Single Guillemot was gently rocking,
In coastal scrub some warblers were flocking.

Next going Eastward, we called at Slapton,
There all kinds of birds our eyes were clapped on,
And was that flat-winged Raptor a Honey?
Well some said, "On that, they'd put their money".

Meanwhile Hirundines skimmed across the Ley,
Whereon afloat were Coot and Goldeneye;
And restless Cetti, that so noisy bird,
With other Warblers too, was seen, and heard.

Start Bay, there some sharp-eyed watchers noted
An active Diver, a nice Black-throated,
But it was so much easier to discern
That Spring arrival, welcome Sandwich Tern.

Birds Northbound, at this time, make their Landfall,
Along the South Coast, so many at Prawle,
We'd sixty species or more, in the day,
Well pleased were we with that vernal display.

DORSET AND HAMPSHIRE DOWNS — June 1994

The Minibus went to a place of renown,
Into deepest Dorset, expectant ever,
We came to a stop on the Battlebush Down,
And to find those good birds was our endeavour.

On top of a hawthorn the Corn Bunting sang,
And also the Skylarks were everywhere heard,
And we wondered, about, how long we would hang
Would it be Montagu's *Tarrier*, that bird?

Above the ripening crop flew the Harrier,
A female Monty on a questing foray,
Was she looking for a male to marry 'er?
But that Lapwing wanted her moved far away.

Then Martin Down, it did not disappoint us,
Though we knew full well they would be hard to see,
Those Stone Curlews, in time, them out, we did suss,
It was a joint effort to find the Thick Knee!

Colourful Lepidopt'ra largely absent,
Well the sun never showed, the scene to lighten,
Blues, Yellows and Reds got expert assessment,
Where many flowers, the Down, up, did brighten.

Resplendent the Yellowhammer posed, a beaut,
Skylarks incessant sang again overall,
Even though there was never an Owl to hoot,
The Turtle Doves puckishly made their catcall!

Of a special hunt were Orchids the subject,
On Burnt Tip, Frog and Bee did some sharp eyes fix,
All in all just the sort of day we expect,
Took more than an instant, but we got the ticks.

FERNWORTHY RESERVOIR/WARREN HOUSE INN — July 1994

We met down there in that Dartmoor hollow,
Fernworthy perimeter to follow,
Avoiding that treacherous mud wallow,
The weather augured well.

We scanned the scene as we skirted the spruce,
Got Corm'rant, Mallard and Canada Goose,
We hoped something good the wood would produce,
Crossbill was much in mind.

Soon there was Chiffchaff, and active Redstart,
Pieds, Siskins and Buzzards all played a part,
A Barnacle Goose then entered the chart,
Swift and Swallow also.

With eager ears we'd awaited the "chip",
But in vain, on Crossbill, out we did dip,
'Nother chance beckoned, next half of the trip,
Off to Warren House Inn.

So across country, B. Three two one two,
Expanse of Dartmoor, spectacular view,
All that and those Hobbies on display too,
Avian theatre.

Two Hobbies passing the time together,
Fast movements, we admired from the heather,
To give perfect sight, conspired the weather,
Red undercarriage clear.

Kestrels were added, and Crossbill it seemed,
Closer inspection and Siskin was deemed,
Transiently, briefly, some eyes had gleamed,
"Wrong" Finch atop that tree.

Of Ring Ousel, Whinchat, we got no sign,
Not on stone outcrop, nor overhead line,
Wheatears and Pipits not so clandestine,
Made themselves evident.

Climbed back to the road, a day to recall,
Watching such Raptors will always enthrall,
Our rapture won't peter out, never pall!
Have bins, will go looking.

PLYMOUTH/TAMAR ESTUARY — December 1994

It was a new venue for the Minibus,
And Terra Incognita for some of us,
As the Tamar Estuary we went to suss,
Weather forecast unfriendly.

First we studied the outfall at Plymouth Hoe,
If there were rare Gulls, for us they did not show,
Not helped by adverse light, cold westerly blow,
We soon made for the ferry.

Torpoint that was where we intended to steer,
As anyone would if they happened to hear,
"In that part of Cornwall there's Desert Wheatear",
A mouth-watering prospect.

Some twitchers were stationed there, fixed to their 'scopes,
And in no time at all, fulfilled were our hopes,
There was the choice vagrant from the Atlas slopes,
So beautifully coloured.

Still drooling, to westward we hit Wacker Creek,
Somewhere was the bird with the utensil beak,
We got the Spoonbill though it played hide-and-seek,
Also were Spotted Redshanks.

So on up the Tamar's west bank to Cargreen,
Where wint'ring Avocets did not stay unseen,
Little Egret was posted there, in between,
Regretfully light near gone.

A memorable trip, quite a list did ensue,
There was general agreement, great bird venue,
Statistical landmark recorded by two,
An annual two hundred.

MINIBUS MEMORIES — 1994

Another good year it was in ninety-four,
And some would be amazed at what birds we saw.
At Chew Valley Lake where we started the year,
There were so many good things out on that mere;
First off we cut our teeth on several Sawbill,
With the number of Duck it was overkill;
We sorted those that dabble from those that dive,
The list soon grew to something like thirty-five,
Not a mild Cheddar, we had a quick gander,
Not to say a fast Goose, and some Goosander,
Next trip was to Slimbridge, braving the hazard,
When on our arrival met by a blizzard;
Then high summer found us on Battlebush Down,
To birders, so often, a place of renown,
Saw jangling Corn Bunting, but we didn't flag,
We wanted "That Raptor" to add to our bag.
At Martin Down where we left no stone unturned,
Until that Curlew we finally discerned,
"Tur, Tur" went the Turtle Doves, doing their turn,
Question — Was it heartbreak, or was it heartburn?
To Bowling Green Marsh, but we had no Jack Snipe,
At Starlings, Peregrine was taking a swipe,
Egyptian Geese, two, were so far from the Nile,
Curlew Sandpiper pleased each *Calidrophile*,
Now a Cormorant had its Plaice in the throng,
That flatfish caused more than a slight contretemps,
There was no chance at all, not even remote,
That the fish could be induced down that bird's throat.
At Exminster, we know that likely we shall,
Hear the Cetti's scolding us by the canal,
December, we thought Christmas early had come,
Torpoint, Desert Wheatear, of year's birds the plum,
Beautiful sandy one had come so far a
Way, maybe from the far distant Sahara.
We'd give the Tamar and Lynher good critique,
And we certainly wouldn't knock Wacker Creek.

Meanwhile we could have stayed put in North Devon,
Late in the year, it became twitchers' heaven,
For into our patch, birders made a beeline,
To see those Warblers in Kenwith's confine,
The Dusky Warbler, hardly in Nature's choir,
But there came many visitors to admire,
Its companion, one with the golden eyebrow,
Far more conspicuous on high willow bough;
Whilst there on the Taw, ripping Velvet Scoter,
Two of them rather exceeded our quota.

SOMERSET LEVELS — January 1995

A lowering sky darkly threatened,
Somerset Levels we were among,
Were speechless to see so much flooding,
Quite dumbfounded, the Catcott our tongue.

Those acres of rheumatic landscape,
Stretching on all sides to the skylines,
We looked for rare Swans in flood meadows,
Also keeping a watch on the rhynes.

Mute Swans could be seen at all quarters,
And Lapwing flocks darkening the sky,
A Finch troop was rising and dropping,
But succeeded in catching our eye.

That gath'ring of Brambling and Chaffinch,
They sought nourishment, scraps from the mud,
We stayed, digesting the spectacle,
While those cattle stood chewing the cud.

Westhay region was much more fruitful,
Far more waterfowl came into view,
Our transport though not amphibious,
Skilfully driven, we made it through.

One well-occupied stretch of water,
We observed from its muddy margins,
Those Duck we had zealously hunted,
Smew and Goosander fell to our bins.

"If you want a good Swan" we were told,
"Proceed that way, past the Cattery",
Sure enough, there it was with some Mutes,
That Whooper earned all our flattery.

Hard astern, so back from the Levels,
Cold and wet, but we didn't complain,
Ornithologic'lly we'd done well,
Our cup ran over, despite the rain.

CORNWALL — February 1995

February's foray,
Minibus meander,
Cornwall called clamantly,
Some six sites scrutinised.

Maer marshy, muddy,
Water was waning well,
Rail recognisable,
Dabbling ducks detected.

Stithians, shivering,
Perpetual Pied-billed,
Rufous Reynard resting,
Graceful grey Goosanders.

Hayle harbouring hundreds,
Gulls gathered generously,
Overt Oystercatchers,
Egret experienced.

Marazion mazy,
Redundant reed-beds ranged,
Blatantly begrudged birds
Choked, chagrined, Cetti-less.

Commodious Carnsew,
Divers duo delight,
Razorbill randomly
Appearing and absent.

Grandiose Godrevy,
Wind whipping white water
Gannets gluttonising,
Sea-splattered Sandpipers

Duchy day dividend,
Some seventy species,
Reliably reckoned,
Memorable medley.

MID-WALES — May 1995
(or "Choughed by Kites, exKited by Choughs!")

Pleasant are Red Kites on high,
Safely, one can prophesy
Barcud you'll see every day,
Twisting tail in the display,
And our spirits soared with them,
Granted avian diadem,
What can with that sight compare,
Not to be seen everywhere.

To Cwmystwyth go and see,
There those Kites they guarantee,
On a sunny forenoon fair,
They will mount the morning air,
Watch enthralled, that rufous bird,
Can't deny your heart is stirred,
Each bird lover must connive
To ensure that Kites will thrive.

Clarach cliffs, the path is rough,
But you'll find the active Chough,
Should you wish, it, to behold
The Welsh coast its last stronghold,
Several Corvids there are found,
Jackdaws, Rooks, and Crows abound,
Ere long shows that scarlet bill,
Recognition, no great skill.

River Rheidol, Nature Trail,
Teal, Goosander, Grey Wagtail,
Redstart, and Flycatcher too,
Hirundines and Buzzard flew,
On then to Tregaron Bog,
Got a varied catalogue,
Whinchat, Warblers, Goldfinch bright,
Swift performing overflight.

Borth where we attention pay
To the sea-birds in the Bay,
Heat haze closes down the range,
Might be Grebes, but ideas change,
R. T. Divers, Sandwich Tern,
They enhance our coast sojourn,
Auks, Mergansers, to and fro,
Manxes, Gannets, great tableau.

Leri Fields and Ynyslas,
Further species we amass,
Among pebbles, among shells,
Birds, Ringed, Aberdovey's belles!
Those small Plovers, yes, they showed,
Then once more we hit the road,
Diverse habitats, we call,
At the Reserve that holds them all.

Ynys-hir, the choice is wide,
This, that, or the other hide,
Birds of woodland, water, field,
Numbers grow to a good yield
Long-tailed Duck, there was a pair,
Of the Cuckoo we're aware,
There's Merganser and Greylag,
Many species "in the bag".

ALPINE FAUNA

When it's summer in the Oberland,
Clothes can be few, and faces fanned,
Whilst eyes are amazed and bins are panned,
Looking for some Swiss species.

High on Planplatten's ridges you may
Attention to the valleys pay,
See Golden Eagles every day,
Majestically soaring.

And from those narrow mountain tracks rough,
You'll see and hear the Alpine Chough,
As flocking, they come across a bluff,
On their search for tourist scraps.

There's no need to be at a great height,
Of two fine Raptors to get sight,
They're of course the Red, and the Black Kite,
Quite common is the latter.

Above the tree line you may descry
Swallowtail, giant butterfly,
A sharp "tsweek" reveals the Snowfinch nigh,
On a seed hunting foray.

With contrasting hues, you'll tell apart
White Wagtail and the Black Redstart;
From a fence the Red-backed Shrike will dart,
It's an up and down feeder.

Nutcrackers with their harsh corvine call,
Can be seen atop spruces tall,
Harder to find Crested Tit so small,
Coniferously concealed.

Ibex and Chamois, high they sojourn,
On precipice they've no concern,
But whistling Marmot you'll soon discern,
Inquisitive on tiptoe.

Delightful Wallcreeper you may trace,
Flying across a bare rock face,
You'll surely never forget that place,
Should you have such good fortune.

As they say, this mentions but a few,
Should the chance come, then go thereto,
Enjoy the fauna, thrill to each view,
There's so much natural beauty.

ONTARIO FALL — 1992

Should you ask me, how was birding,
In the Fall, Canadian Autumn,
In Ontario's southern margin,
By the Lake named as the Province,
Sister of the Gitche Gumee,
Vasty, shining big sea water?
I shall answer, I shall tell you,
"But a tiny patch was birded,
Weighed against the myriad acres
Of that huge expansive Province,
But the Lake-side Park of Presqu'ile,
Diverse habitats provided,
There were reed-beds by the acre,
There Shuh-shuh-gah, Great Blue Heron,
Stood obliging in the channel,
Ere with monstrous wings expanded,
Flew it into heavy cover.
Red-winged Blackbirds called together,
Now in reeds and now in tree top;
Whilst the Pied-billed Grebe so active,
Diving now, then showing clearly;
Came also its cousin, Red-necked,
And the Horned one as they call it,
Which to us is the Slavonian.
On the Lake, and in the marshes,
Varied Species drew attention,
There were Loon, Great Northern Divers
As we call them, here in Britain,
Double-crested Cormorants swarthy,
And the Geese named as their homeland,
Whilst the Duck in some profusion,
Covered quite a lot of water,
Flocks of Scoter, they call White-winged,
Which we know best as the Velvet,
Mallard, Pintail, Gadwall, Wigeon,
Shoveler, Teal of Green-winged sub-group,
Their Mergansers, our Goosanders,
With the Goldeneye were diving,

Are you back at home you wonder,
Seeing such familiar Species?
Then came Black Duck, Scaup the Lesser,
Ring-necked Duck and Bufflehead came,
With the Transatlantic Wigeon.
So to turn from open water,
Gave our best and close attention
To the beach, the Lake-side margin,
Where the sand was gently shelving,
And the tangly seaweed patches
Proved inviting to the shore-birds,
Also known to us as Waders
There was Chetowaik the Plover,
Onomatopoeic Killdeer,
Some Black-bellied ones, Grey Plover,
As they're known to us in Britain,
Plover small, Semi-palmated,
Our old friends the Dunlin scampered,
With the Sanderling so busy,
Other Sandpipers too visit,
Came the Least, Semi-palmated,
Also White-rumped swelled the Species.
Ruddy Turnstones to Canadians,
But we drop the mild expletive!
And to us they are just Turnstones,
There were other treats, and rare ones,
Came Hudsonian, rare Godwit,
Briefly visited the shoreline,
Stood, then flew along the shoreline;
Then loud calling, like a Greenshank,
Greater Yellowlegs, three flew in,
Whilst we gazed with admiration,
At the close-up of that trio,
Was that almost worth the air fare?
Next a Phalarope, the Red-necked,
Finely spun the shallow water,
Followed later, three days later,
By the Red one, we call Grey one,
Gulls there were, they paid a visit,
Bonaparte's and Ring-billed mainly,

Herring Gulls were also spotted,
Now for scrub, and now for woodland,
Inland from the widespread waters,
Passerines were coming, going,
When revealed, we saw the Sparrows,
Saw the Song one, saw the Swamp one,
And the White-crowned, and the Tree one,
Downy Woodpecker quite tiny,
Then a Nuthatch, the White-breasted,
Kinglets, two denominations,
Active were among the branches,
Grounded House Wren in the bushes,
Whilst Brown Creeper round the trunk went,
And the Veery liked its cover,
Dark-eyed Juncos flocking, flitting,
Eastern Meadowlark, bright, calling,
Warblers, Yellow-rumped and others,
Hawks the Sharp-shinned and the Cooper's,
And the Red-tailed too was present,
All in contrast to the Monarch,
Golden Butterfly migrating,
Like so many birds migrating,
To a warmer winter, southwards,
Into Mexico, well southward,
Duck, the Redhead, and the Moorhen,
Crow American quite common,
E. & O. E., 'twas the picture
Of the Presqu'ile Park at Brighton,
Garden species now to mention,
Blue Jays everywhere and noisy,
Mourning Doves and Eastern Phoebes,
Perched the fences, and the branches,
Came also American Robin,
Upright, waiting for the earthworms,
Black-capped Chickadees so fearless,
And his Eminence the Cardinal,
Honoured us that day at Cobourg,
Brilliant Red but for black visage,
Joined his minions, garden feeding."
Should you wonder, should you ask me,

Were there still more birds about there?
I shall answer, I shall tell you.
"From a country road were sighted
Turkey Vultures, two together,
Great long wings have they the Vultures,
They disturbed a crowd of Crows or
Maybe it was vice versa,
Roadside views there were of Cowbird,
Swallows a large flock was resting,
Wires supporting the Tree Swallows,
Unconcerned in a small pond there,
Stood a Yellowlegs, the Lesser,
Whilst a Kingfisher, the Belted,
Shot across the Lake called Little,
Quite the largest concentration
Of the Gulls was in a meadow,
Several hundred were there roosting,
Goodrich-Loomis, country park is,
Where we missed the Ruffèd Grouses,
But the Chickadees and Juncos,
With a Pewee and some Blue Jays,
Also Red-tailed Hawk, were added,
These were clearly close in vision,
But the ones that most delighted,
Were the Bluebirds, Eastern Bluebirds,
Richly hued, the Autumn found them,
Peering into nesting boxes,
Booking Spring accommodation?
Yet more venues, yet more sightings,
With a Swan, in New York State seen,
In canal just by the roadside,
But discovery was imperfect,
Was it Mute or was it Tundra?
Grackle most obliging, tree perched,
Looking like an all-dark Magpie,
Also in short US visit,
Double Crested Cormorant showed up,
As did the familiar Mallard,
Bonaparte's Gull there were several,
In that Fall, the Falls Niagara,

Were the haunt of Gulls in plenty,
Ring-billed, Bonaparte's and Herring,
And the Chickadees were lively,
Whilst the Humming Bird, Peruvian,
Kept within the tropic greenhouse,
Then the House Sparrows familiar,
Hardly overlooked could they be."
You may wonder, you may ask me
Are still others to be mentioned?
I shall tell you, I shall answer.
"Cobourg Harbour held some Snow Geese,
Blue phase immature, the Snow Geese,
Canadas were also present,
And of Gulls, the Great Black-backed ones,
With the Herring, and the Ring-billed,
Out upon the Lake's wide water
Cruised the Loon, and Grebe the Hornèd,
Starlings here and also elsewhere,
Saw the House Finch share an aerial,
Share a television aerial,
With a Mourning Dove and Robin,
Out at Goodrich was the Redpoll,
Whilst a Pheasant called from cover
Then at Cramahe, in the country,
Goldfinches American flew,
With some Sparrows in the scrub there,
On a farm, keeping low profile,
Was the Chukar type of Partridge,
Over woodland near Trent River,
Flew the Mockingbird so soundful."
If still further you should ask me,
What of animals were sighted?
I should answer, I should tell you.
"Chipmunks agile, came to gardens,
Handsome creatures, hungry creatures,
And quite common were the Squirrels,
Red were some, whilst black were others,
Yet again, of course, the gray ones,
And the residential Beaver,
Hiawatha's Ahmeek, hiding,

Didn't show, we saw the signs there,
Where rude carpentry had felled trees,
Gnawed through boles, a lodge to fashion,
Keep in touch those busy Beavers
With their trunk calls in the forest!
On the ground, amongst leaf litter,
Slid and slithered, pale striped greenish,
Garter Snake with red tongue darting."
In that Fall the trees resplendent,
Specially so the blazing Maples,
So the holiday was ended,
But come Spring, and comes the promise
Of return, to catch the bird life
Turning north again, so many,
Others nesting near the Lake-side,
So a change of season bringing
Fresh delights for happy birders.

ONTARIO SPRING — 1993

Came the Spring, returned the birder,
To the north shore of that water,
To Ontario's Lakeside, stretching,
Miles and miles with scrub and trees there,
So providing sheltered roosting
For the avian migrants northing
From their habitats in winter,
From that temperate, gentle, winter
Of the Gulf, and even souther.
Hardier residents surviving
Arctic temperatures subzero,
Now give thought to nesting, mating,
Whilst the snow-melt raised the level,
Water in profusion greater,
Spread around, more pools and lakelets,
Adding to the many shallows
Where the Blue-winged Teal were dodging
In and out of weeds and grasses,
Solitary the Sandpiper,
As the name, so no companions,
Happily it stayed quite closely,
Also Presqu'ile's further bonus,
Came that big white bird, Great Egret,
Dropping down inside a reed-bed,
And so audible the Geese Skeins,
Daytime, night-time ever calling,
Making northward for the summer;
Whilst the Caspian Terns were fishing,
Big red bills have they for fishing.
Falling low the sun at Presqu'ile,
When, announcing their arrival,
Lesser Yellowlegs, a pair came,
Calling loudly, staying briefly,
So unlike the Red-winged Blackbirds,
Ever present, ever singing,
As the Lake water receded,
Showing shingle, showing sandbank,
Massed the Gulls of different species,

Bonaparte's, Herring, and Ring-billed,
Great Black-backed and Terns, the Common,
And the Caspian, finding room there,
Seeking space from crowded island,
Where were hundreds of them nesting,
And the mingled cries incessant,
Carried to the shore, some distance,
Dunlin, Killdeer, joined the bird throng,
Whilst the trees provided refuge
For the migrants, birds of passage,
Warblers, Yellow-rumped and Yellow,
With Black-throated Blue arriving,
And Magnolia also showing,
Sparrows various, Grackle, Cowbird,
And the Flycatchers so varied,
From the Least to the Great Crested,
Northern Oriole fluting sweetly,
Flashing red, and flashing orange,
And the contrast of the colours
Worn by Bobolink and Grosbeak,
Also on the Lake at Presqu'ile
There were Brant, it's said two thousand,
Line ahead in a huge convoy,
Ducks the Oldsquaw, and the Ring-necked,
Great assembly of Merganser,
Bufflehead and some Surf Scoter,
Common Loon, just one was sighted,
Whilst the Pied-billed Grebe were nesting,
Now emerging from the reed-beds,
Then returning, back in hiding;
But the Kingfisher, the Belted,
Prominently perched on look-out,
Short shrift to the fish was threat'ning,
Call proclaiming Common Flicker,
Loud repeated call announced it,
Whilst the Downy and the Hairy,
More discreet of the Woodpeckers,
Made their presence not so obvious,
But the giant of the Order,
The Pileated was elusive,

Found the excavated tree trunk,
Heard the noisy clam'rous cackle,
But the perpetrator vanished.
Well seen the delightful Hummers,
Dainty, tiny, Ruby-throated,
Whirring wings defy the eyesight,
Sipping energising nectar,
Swallows various, some advantaged
By provision of nest boxes.
To the Lone Pine Marsh in Cramahe,
Where our visit coincided
With a pole-squatting large Raptor,
Legs so darkly, deeply feathered,
Maybe immature Bald Eagle;
Also Doves and Red-winged Blackbirds,
And a Grosbeak, the Rose-breasted,
What time frogs croaked so persistent,
Should you wonder, should you ask me,
Of those days, which was the best one,
I shall answer, I shall tell you,
"That it was the day we joined a
Field excursion, travelling eastward,
To remote Prince Edward County,
To the very point Prince Edward,
On this wooded promontary,
There we saw the migrant Warblers,
Saw the Black and White, the Gold-winged
Also Nashville with the Yellow,
Cape May, Yellow-rumped, Magnolia,
And Black-throated Green and Blue too,
Chestnut-sided with Blackburnian,
Also Palm, and the Bay-breasted,
With the transatlantic Redstart,
Perched were all in leafless branches,
Of the Hickory trees so twisted,
So we had a visual vantage,
And saw well polychrome chorus,
Vying also for attention,
Buntings, Indigo so splendid,
Oriole, Bobolink, and Grosbeak,

In a marsh our eyes were gladdened
By Green Heron, and by Bittern.
Standing still among the Cat-tails,
Whilst the Woodcock camouflaged well
Yet escaped not keen-eyed watcher.
Blue-winged Teal, Oldsquaw were added,
With some Hawks and Turkey Vultures,
Swallows, Flycatchers so various,
Kingbirds, Phoebes, East Wood Pewee,
White-throat Sparrows, Killdeer Plovers,
Ring-billed Gulls, Brown Thrasher also,
Purple Martin, Catbird, House Wren,
So, reluctant, back to westward,
Next p.m. we're found at Brighton,
At Lagoon so chill and windswept,
But Black Tern and Rusty Blackbird,
Spotted Sandpiper and Oldsquaw,
Lesser Scaup, Redhead, and Flicker,
Noteworthy among the birdlife,
And atop a reed heap, stirring,
Was a lumb'ring Snapping Turtle,
Fearsome beast the Snapping Turtle,
Will seize avidly the wildfowl,
Maybe Turtle eggs would hatch there,
Inside reeded incubator.
Other birdlife not yet mentioned,
But most worthy of attention,
Seen in town, and seen in country,
Were the Meadowlark and Bluebird,
Scarlet Tanager and Junco,
And the Rufous-sided Towhee,
Black-capped Chickadee and Blue Jay,
Northern Harrier, our Hen Harrier,
And among the other wildlife,
Dead Racoon, a highway victim,
Beaver and the Beaver lodges,
White-tailed Deer, Red Fox and Groundhog,
Squirrels, Red, and Black, and Gray ones,
One Spring day this very birder,
With his colleague, they rose early,

Well before the sun was showing,
Left behind a sleeping Colborne
Early morning darkness lingered
When they reached the park at Presqu'ile,
Settled by the marsh at Presqu'ile,
Near the entrance to the boardwalk,
Saw the sun climb the horizon,
Saw light steal across the water,
And chill yielded to Spring sunshine,
Greeted by Blackbird and Robin,
White-crowned Sparrow, Yellow Warbler,
Pied-billed Grebe and Great Blue Heron,
Caspian Tern and also House Wren
Sang its heart out, sang unceasing,
White-tailed Deer emerged from woodland,
And at leisure crossed the tarmac,
Later Kinglet, Towhee, Grosbeak,
Warblers, Yellow-rumped, Magnolia,
Chickadee and Northern Oriole,
And the Lake, as well, provided,
Common Tern and few Surf Scoter.
So the holiday was ended,
But the memory still lingers,
Of Canadian bird bonanza."

ONTARIO SPRING — 1994

One year on, returned the birder,
Back to Canada's wide spaces,
To Ontario's open country,
Once again the Spring migration
Was a strong call, northward movement,
Of the birds that wintered warmly,
Came to seek them, came to find them,
Near the Lake shore of great water,
Lake Ontario's north coast, border,
Looking south beyond horizon
Lies the USA, whence travelled
Migrants flying in huge numbers;
Presqu'ile Park regular landfall,
Temporary rest for many,
Ere resuming further travel,
Though for some their breeding places
Are right there, right there in Presqu'ile;
There were Cormorants, Double-crested,
Solitary Loon was showing,
As were Mallard, Gadwall, Scoter,
Ring-necked Duck, Hooded Merganser,
Scaup the Lesser, and the Greater,
Oldsquaw, Red-breasted Merganser;
In the end, down by the lighthouse,
Saw the Harlequin pair closely,
Of the Duck the most elusive,
Harlequins that drew the twitchers,
Bufflehead were there in numbers,
And a Ruddy Duck, a single.
Great Blue Heron stalked the marshes,
And at dusk the Black-crowned Night one,
Motionless inside a reed-bed,
And one evening heard the Bittern,
Then emerged the New World Bittern,
Flying near, above the cat-tails.
Heard and saw the noisy Marsh Wren,
Then Virginia Rails were sounding,
Saw them running through the reed stems,

Pied-billed Grebe were intermittent,
Sometimes there and sometimes hiding,
Transatlantic Coot, a few showed,
From across the Lake, Sandpipers,
Those Sandpipers were the Spotted;
On the windswept beach the Dunlin,
With the Gulls, Herring and Ring-billed,
Bonaparte's and the Great Black backed,
Active Terns too, busy feeding,
Were the Caspian and the Common,
And exploding from the roadside,
In the evening shade, a Woodcock,
From some marshy ground the Woodcock,
Calling as it went a-roding.
You may wonder, you may ask me
What of land birds, I shall tell you,
"At Presqu'ile so many species,
Sharp-shinned Hawk, its tail betrayed it,
As it circled ever watchful,
Mourning Dove of doleful calling,
Humming Bird, the Ruby-throated,
Sitting motionless half hidden,
Tiny jewel in the foliage.
Belted Kingfisher quite raucous,
Once seen sampling pond in woodland,
Quite a tiny pond in woodland,
Hurried glimpse of great Woodpecker,
The Pileated, like steam hammer
Gouges out great holes in tree trunks.
Other Woodpeckers, the Hairy,
And the Downy, tiny Downy,
Also Flycatchers so different,
Eastern Kingbird, Eastern Phoebe,
And the Least, distinctive caller
Loud and clear "CHE-BEK" is sounded,
Then Great-crested, somewhat larger,
With a rusty tail Great Crested.
Very active were the Swallows,

The Barn Swallow, The Tree Swallow,
With the larger Purple Martin
In the multi-celled nest boxes.
Through the trees the rowdy Blue Jay,
Then the hoarse croak of the Raven,
Then the Crow its smaller cousin,
Much more numerous than the Raven,
Like the Chickadee, Black-capped one,
But the Nuthatch, the Red-breasted,
Only made but one appearance,
Twice as many the Brown Creeper,
Of our Treecreeper the image,
Saw the House Wren busy nesting,
Busy nesting in a tree stump,
Richly rufous the Brown Thrasher,
With its tail so elongated.
So abundant was the Robin,
And an opportunist nester.
On a low branch sat the Wood Thrush,
Chunky, spotted, large the Wood Thrush,
In Jobes Wood, a part of Presqu'ile,
Was a Thrush, the one called Swainson's,
Whilst a Veery showed quite tamely,
We were there with full moon shining,
Trying to entice a Barred Owl,
This by hopefully repeating
An approximation of the
Hooting call, but luck not with us,
We were ignored studiously,
Save by many frogs that mocked us,
And by ravenous mosquitoes.
On the wet ground in the woodland,
There the Waterthrush was feeding,
Though so named, it is a Warbler.
Also Gnatcatcher, the Blue Gray,
In a shrubbery prospected,
Watched a Kinglet, Ruby-crowned one,
And the European Starling,
Quite at home across the ocean,
Red-winged Blackbird very many,

Presence heard continuously,
Common Grackle, Brown-head Cowbird,
Both abundant, with the latter
Laying eggs in nests of others,
Copying the Old World Cuckoo,
Northern Oriole, lovely, tuneful,
And the Tanager, bright scarlet,
Evening Grosbeak, one infrequent,
With its green bill, was a prize one;
The Rose-breasted also present,
Not so scarce this other Grosbeak,
And amongst the several Sparrows,
There the Chipping, Swamp, Savannah,
Song, White-throated, and the White-crowned."
What birds came into the gardens,
You may ask me, I shall tell you,
"In bad weather, Ring-billed Gulls came,
Mourning Doves with tails long, pointed,
Took the sunflower seed with pleasure,
The delightful Ruby-throated
Humming Bird came to the feeders,
Took the sugar/water mixture,
Common Flickers scoured grass patches,
Hunting ants, a staple diet;
Other Woodpeckers, the Downy
Hammered at the garden Maples,
Also Kingbird and the Phoebe
Looked for flies, but Chickadees were
Active, constant at the feeders,
Brilliant Goldfinch, and the House Finch,
And the Purple Finch, they gorged seed,
The House Sparrow fewer of them,
Gath'ring crumbs the Red-winged Blackbirds,
And seeds fallen from the tables,
With the Common Grackle also,
And the Cowbird, the Brown-headed.
Gracing us with an appearance,
Cardinal there, robed in scarlet,
And the perky Chipping Sparrow,
In a rainstorm, a Pine Grosbeak

Tarried at the garden feeder.
At the Lone Pine Marsh in Cramahe,
A few visits were rewarding,
To this rural roadside haven,
Acres eighty-six in all there,
In this hunt-free sanctuary,
Ring-necked Duck showed up and Wood Duck,
Mallard not quite unexpected,
Belted Kingfisher persistent,
Hardly "belted up", so noisy,
Also present, no doubt breeding,
Were the Canadas, big grey geese,
Came a Gray Jay, and a Blue Jay,
And Rose-breasted Grosbeak, whistling,
In the marsh were Red-winged Blackbirds,
The odd European Starling,
Busy Woodpeckers tree climbing,
Both the Downy and the Hairy,
Chickadees were there, tree flitting,
Killdeer occupied a roadside,
And Tree Swallows hawked the wetland,
Red-tailed Hawk, it came exploring,
But it was a curtailed visit;
Porcupine, a traffic victim,
Lay beside a fence immobile;
Swimming Beaver, or a Muskrat,
Briefly showed, head above water,
Cobourg Harbour gets next mention,
Blowing chill it was that May day,
Well disturbed the choppy water,
And the Cormorants, Double-crested,
Some two hundred flocked together
Restless moved they round the harbour,
And out on the Lake unsettled,
In their company, a large Gull,
Huge white Glaucous, second year one,
On the harbour walls, and water,
Many other Gulls, the Ring-billed,
And the Bonaparte's in numbers,
With a Caspian Tern, an odd one,

Keeping wary distance from us,
On rough ground a Killdeer Plover,
Introduced itself but briefly,
Swallows skimming low were many,
Next place the lagoon at Brighton,
Lesser Scaup and pair of Shoveler,
Native Geese and Red-winged Blackbird,
Once again Tree Swallows active,
Also Chipping Sparrow, Phoebe,
But reported Cattle Egret,
Proved elusive, did not find it.
Eastward one day, rainy morning,
Reached the bird place, there at Wooler,
There amid the farming country,
Shown the clutch inside a bird box,
Where the Eastern Bluebird nested,
Never far away the Bluebirds,
Great Blue Heron cruised above us,
Yellow Warbler, Phoebe calling,
Meadowlark, Tree Swallow, Rock Dove.
Had warm afternoon at Goodrich,
At reserve called Goodrich-Loomis,
Watched that Woodpecker, the Flicker,
Pecking at the ground for ant fare,
In a tree, Yellow-rumped Warbler,
Softly singing, whilst the Blue Jay,
Hardly could be overlooked there,
And Brown Thrasher, and a Phoebe,
Showed well with Rock Dove and Robin,
Voluble the Red winged Blackbirds,
Quiet the Mallard in the streamlet,
Found the Trillium in the woodland,
Found that flower, Provincial emblem,
Found the white one, found the red one.
Good friends drove us, a day's birding,
Campbellford on the Trent River,
Where we stopped and made acquaintance
With the Ospreys, nesting Ospreys,
Nested on a raised, high platform,
Inside tall surrounding fencing

Of a generating station.
In the area more Swallows,
There were Bank ones, also Barn ones,
Travelling on we found Crowe River,
Flowing fast it was, Crowe River,
Here we saw a White-crowned Sparrow,
Yet more Swallows and a Grackle.
On to Twin Lakes, more swift water,
Getting to Laurentian Country,
Where geology has altered,
Gone the Limestone, now find granite,
Great outcrops of granite boulders.
Red-winged Blackbird, Rusty Blackbird,
And a Robin, and a Flicker,
With Song Sparrow and Brown Thrasher;
Overhead a Raven floated.
In the trees at edge of roadside,
Perched a pair of Turkey Vultures,
Ugly, scavengers, red-headed,
Maybe nesting, so, we wondered,
Petroglyphs Provincial Park was
Our next stop, the weather closing,
Scarcely was there time to listen
To that Warbler in the pine trees,
Shiv'ring call, Northern Parula,
When the storm broke, heavy rainfall,
Thunder, lightning, and hail also,
So to end a day remembered.
Visited some friends at Smithfield,
Set in fields their house at Smithfield,
Watched arrivals at their feeders,
Came the Purple, and the House Finch,
Came the Ruby-throated Hummer,
With the Goldfinch and the Bluc Jay,
Chickadees participating,
Downy Woodpecker and Grackle,
Northern Oriole and Rock Dove,
In low flight a Northern Harrier
Quartered neighb'ring field intently,
Overflying were two Killdeer,

Also Ring-billed Gulls were present.
Came the day, the annual outing,
Of the Presqu'ile-Brighton birders,
To the famed Prince Edward County,
There to study Spring migration
Of the Warblers, of the others,
North across the Lake from Stateside.
A wet start we had from Brighton,
Twenty something in the party,
Later came some better weather,
First to itemise the Warblers,
Black and White, Northern Parula,
Sev'ral Yellow and one Hooded,
Chestnut-sided, and Bay-breasted,
Yellowthroat, and two Blackburnian,
A few Transatlantic Redstart,
Ovenbird and the Magnolia,
Also Yellow-rumped, a few there,
And Black-throated Green, and Blue there,
That's the record of the Warblers,
From its roosting branch was flushed a,
Whip-poor-will, it soon departed,
Scarlet Tanagers glowed brightly,
Midst the scrub and midst the bushes,
Whilst the Northern Orioles shone
On the, as yet, unleaved branches,
As did Grosbeaks, the Rose-breasted,
And the Evening one was showing;
Different Flycatchers we noted,
Eastern Kingbird, Eastern Phoebe,
With Great-crested and the Least one,
Chickadee, House Wren, Gray Catbird,
Latter with its feline mewing,
Crow, American, and Robin,
Blue Jay, European Starling,
Bright yellow the native Goldfinch,
Crimson markings on the House Finch,
And deep blue, Indigo Bunting;
Came the Rufous-sided Towhee,
And four Sparrows, first the White-crowned,

Then the Song one, and the Chipping,
Next Savannah, a short-tailed one,
Red-winged Blackbird, Common Grackle,
Also Meadowlark and Veery,
Red-tailed Hawk and Northern Harrier,
On and near the Lake, and marshland,
Canada Geese, they were not absent,
Flocked the Swallows, Tree ones, Barn ones,
And the Cliff ones were mud nesting
On the ancient wooden lighthouse;
Northern Rough-winged Swallows also,
Finding banks to make a nest in;
Oldsquaw, Red-breasted Merganser,
Gulls, the Great Black-backed and Ring-billed,
And some Herring Gulls were showing,
Saw the ever-present Mallard,
Blue-winged Teal and Northern Pintail,
Sandpipers, the Solitary,
But a pair beside a marsh pool,
Almost blue their legs appearing,
Double-crested Cormorants also.
And a careless Ruffed Grouse crossing,
Nearly got itself run over
White-tailed Deer that quickly vanished
Garter snake slid through the leaf mould.
Out at Cramahe, near the Highway,
Torrid was the afternoon then,
Round the scrub the Eastern Kingbird,
And a Meadowlark were showing,
Bobolink and Red-winged Blackbird,
From a willow, East Wood Pewee
Sang its own peculiar lyric,
Nearby "PETER! PETER! PETER!"
Rang out from a Tufted Titmouse.
Chipping Sparrows and some Robins,
With Tree Swallows swelled the numbers.
Meanwhile Black flies and Mosquitoes
Took too great a fancy to us,
And we missed those big Wild Turkeys,
Said to be around that district.

But next evening sought the Nighthawk,
Sought the Chimney Swift at twilight,
Drove to Brighton, sat in car park,
There, awaiting their appearance,
Soon came Chimney Swifts and Starlings,
But the Common Nighthawk shunned us,
Once again our good friends drove us
For a day spent near the Rice Lake;
At Gores Landing, there the first stop,
There saw Chickadee and Blackbird,
Serpent Mounds, we reached there later,
A Provincial Park, extensive,
Bordering the shore of Rice Lake,
Great Blue Heron crossed the water,
Spotted Sandpipers showed briefly,
As along the bank they journeyed,
And the Swallows were abundant,
A Goose family kept their distance,
Orioles, one or two showing,
And Flycatcher, Olive-sided,
Red-eyed Vireo and Grackle
Warbler, Yellow-rumped, and Robin,
And the Kingbird and the Starling.
Coming back, along the Lakeside,
Near the road, a Common Loon stayed,
And the Red-breasted Merganser,
Of which plenty, sometimes diving,
Never far away the Mallard,
Gulls Ring-billed and the Great Black-backed,
Several Terns also were passing,
Common, Caspian, were passing,
Came the last day of vacation,
Went back looking for the Turkeys,
Went back to the wood at Smithfield,
And this time we heard their gobbles,
But the thick scrub kept them hidden,
And for us the time was pressing,
So, alas the birding ended.

BIRDSONG

The verses on each page of this Section may be sung to the tune of a familiar song or hymn. Titles are shown at the end of each poem.

SAWBILLS

Some talk of the Goosander,
And some applaud the Smew,
The Red-breasted Merganser
Has its supporters too,
They're a most attractive trio
That catch aquatic fare,
Those so expert fishing Sawbills,
Sea ducks quite beyond compare.

In the most wintry weather
You will see all inland
On reservoir or pits, there
Can be a largish band;
The massed colour, grace and beauty
An overwhelming sight,
It's an angling club quite peerless,
They will always get a bite.

Now watch a moving squadron,
A lake where cold winds blow,
Now hidden by the wavelets,
Now plunging down below,
Or in some rough coastal waters,
They feed most happ'ly still,
There's no fish will ever break free
From that tight serrated bill.

"The British Grenadiers"

GREAT CRESTED GREBES

Great Crested Grebes are bonny
When in their breeding dress,
And their display when courting,
It really does impress
It really does impress,
They shake their heads in glee,
They offer weeds from underwater,
It's quite something to see.

They breed by inland water,
Afloat, the nest is moored,
And soon after the hatching
The young may be "aboard",
The young may be "aboard",
They ride free of alarm,
On the parents' backs they travel safely,
Avoiding *grebous* harm!

"Annie Laurie"

ENDANGERED SPECIES

It's troubling, great pity,
That's the theme of this ditty,
That some birds are scarcer than they used to be,
Take the Partridge and Eider,
You have to search wider,
Before you can find them in the field or at sea,
In the field or at sea,
In the field or at sea,
They're harder to find in the field or at sea.

It's just symptomatic,
We can say this emphatic,
The environment's suffering, pollutions abound,
Wholesale changes in farming,
Brought results alarming,
Has it been left too late to recover lost ground?
Recover lost ground,
Recover lost ground,
Now it could be too late to recover lost ground.

"Cockles and Mussels"

HARTLAND POINT/MAER LAKE — September 1988

At Hartland they're ringing, the birds they're not singing,
And neither would you be if caught in a net,
Those two Kestrels playing, they seem to be saying,
"It's your turn to hover, I'll catch you, I bet."
With friends from Okehampton we are getting damped on,
But though the rain eases it's rather misty,
We scarcely see Lundy, let's all come back Monday,
It just might be better for watching the sea.

The haze is receding, we see Gannets feeding,
Piscatory appetites second to none,
Dive Cormorants under, and Shags join the plunder,
Aquatic existence is not always fun;
There's that Peregrine, still, has fed well from a kill,
It sits there disdainfully, is it awake?
So we're now in a mood to be thinking of food,
It's back to the cars for a timely lunch break.

And when Hartland we'd viewed, we proceeded to Bude.
We reached Maer Lake, there were Waders on show,
And some eyes had a glint as they saw Little Stint,
Together with Redshank, the Spotted you know,
Then the species list grew with Godwit and Curlew,
The reed-beds were teeming with Duck, mainly Teal,
With a most careful glance you could see Jack Snipe dance,
Rare Sandpipers too can add to the appeal.

"The Ash Grove"

FREMINGTON PILL/ISLEY MARSH — November 1988
(or "Up the creek without fiddle-faddle")

Fremington Pill,
Not bitter one to swallow,
Bird-watching hopes can oftentimes high soar,
Sandpipers various came to our attention,
Before we reached the estuary of Taw,
A Kingfisher delighted us by perching,
Fishing for food, or for our compliments,
Then westerly we turned along the foreshore,
Getting frustrated by the elements.

Turnstones were there,
And Little Grebe and Greenshank,
Godwit Bar-tailed, and Oystercatchers too,
Some active Dunlin skimmed across the water,
Whilst Teal and Wigeon we could dimly view,
With thoughts of big white birds we pressed to Isley,
Could we get there before it turned to night?
Well, yes we did and what is more those Spoonbills
Flew into view, we got a lovely sight.

Oh Isley Marsh,
You're thought of very Isley,
RSPB have purchased there some land,
We always visit you with expectation,
For Fowl and Waders you can beat the band;
Your ornithology can draw the twitcher,
For Short-eared Owl, and Egret and so on,
But all the same one can be disappointed,
Egretfully go there and find them — gone.

"Londonderry Air"

BROWNSHAM WOODS — May 1992
(or "It's a Sylvia, but what is she?")

If you go down to the woods today,
At Brownsham, you'll get a surprise,
For birds don't always sing as they should,
They're sometimes taking a rise;
The Garden Warbler, would you believe,
When singing can so eas'ly deceive,
And you will say "Can anyone see that Blackcap?"
They like hiding in the scrub,
Just a tiny glimpse is what you'll see,
Leaves move as they search for grub,
So which one is it now, can you agree?
If you're patient then you might
Catch the Sylvia Warbler unaware,
Unless you're blessed with very good hearing,
A sighting you must get,
That's a Blackcap, but can you swear?

Then out of the wood, we scaled a cliff,
Up a zigzag path, not flat,
Keeping us company on the climb,
Was a nice pair of Stonechat,
Beneath some trees we sat on a bank,
'Twas picnic time, we ate and we drank,
Before the return arboreal was tackled;
Nuthatches played hide-and-seek,
Foliage foiled finding faintly few,
So we could have stayed a week,
And yet still had a rather hazy view,
Garden Warblers teased again,
One, at last was seen, did not escape,
By then we're nearly back at the car park,
Home well in time for tea,
To play, once more, that Birdsong tape.

"Teddy Bears' Picnic"

THE NORTH DEVON SURF SCOTER — January 1992

Ilfracombe yes, Ilfracombe yes,
Ilfracombe that's where you came,
A Surf Scoter, a rare floater,
Now you're in the Hall of Fame.

Chorus — Oh my Scoter, Oh my Scoter,
You have wandered far from home,
Near the coastline, how you show fine,
Stay awhile, ere off you roam.

You're a black drake, you're a black drake,
With a heavy coloured bill,
Welcome scarce guest from the far west,
You're a tick for which we'd kill.

Came the twitchers, Came the twitchers,
To North Devon's cliffs so tall,
Such a good view, they could see you,
From behind the car park wall.

"Clementine"

J

GO FIND A KITE

Why there's no sight of the Red Kite,
Can such a loss e'er be put right?
Once it was found extensively,
In London streets it used to be.

Now just in Wales it never fails,
Seen there in flocks, and that's not tales,
Resident there the numbers grow,
But needs surveillance even so.

Find a Red Kite, search with your might,
It's so rewarding seen in flight,
Should you see one it's sure to be
Bird of the year most certainly.

Milvus Milvus is worth a fuss,
Must get it right, can't miss the bus,
Kite conservation must not fail,
No unforeseen "twist in the tale".

"Fight the Good Fight"

TRANSATLANTIC TOURISTS

Sandpipers fly over the ocean,
American shorebirds they do,
The Yellowlegs, Baird's and the Western,
Buff-breasted and Dowitcher too,
They come, They come,
There's not so many, but some appear,
A few, A few,
Will turn up quite reg'lar each year.

Just one on its own, not unusual,
Blown thousands of miles off its course,
And when it is put on the Birdline,
The twitchers arrive there in force,
From near, From far,
Birders make sure that it won't be missed,
One more, One more,
For a lifer, or annual list.

Now some they will stay over Winter,
Whilst others you scarcely can meet,
Like some of those overseas tourists,
Grass doesn't grow under their feet,
Yankees, Yankees,
It's in the Fall, that's when they descend,
Make sure, Make sure,
Make sure that your list you extend.

Identification is tricky,
You must get good views to be sure
Comparing the wing with the tail length,
Is it equal, or less, is it more?
Eye stripe, Eye ring,
There can be differences so small
Bill shape, Bill size,
Failing all else there's the call.

So think of that poor little Wader,
Making south, for the Gulf, and beyond,
And missing the Sea Caribbean,
But braving the wide "Herring Pond"
At sea, At sea,
All at sea, it must be feeling sick
Wand'ring, Wand'ring,
Just to give us all a tick.

"My Bonnie is Over the Ocean"

COULD ALWAYS GET YOU A TAME PET-SHOP MYNAH

I'd like to get you a nice vagrant from China,
All for yourself alone,
Get you a lifer, a great mega-tick,
Leaving the others feeling just a little bit sick;
A Grey-necked Bunting,
Would have twitchers hunting,
Or Dusky Warbler say,
I'd like to get you a nice vagrant from China,
All for yourself some day.

Maybe I'll get you on a slow boat to Lundy,
Just us, and two hundred more,
We could get lucky, do you want to bet?
Over the side, look, that could be the Murrelet,
The Oldenburg's churning,
With twin screws fast turning,
Could be a trip to recall,
Don't think it's all flannel in the Bristol Channel,
Never a story too tall.

But these I can't get you, I'm no bird diviner,
We'd have to try Birdline,
Watchers all over there are taking stock,
Some of them travelling all around the bloomin' clock,
But not to worry,
'Cos you're in no hurry,
Can't dash off looking for plums,
Your list could be richer, but then you're no twitcher,
Taking each day as it comes.

"Slow Boat to China"

FEW OF MY FUNLINES

The other day, clear, I saw it quite near,
From Hartland Lighthouse, it came across,
Enormous sea-bird, no, not a Gannet,
It was more like an Albatross.

The other evening, as I was peeping
Between the curtains, the moon shone bright,
I saw a Barn Owl, it started screeching,
Don't know who had the greater fright.

A household feline will make a beeline,
For garden birds, and if those you love,
Don't let the cat get among the Pigeons,
Unless you want a Collared Dove!

So in the sunshine, or in the moonlight,
The birds are out there, yes, never fear,
Into thick bushes, or into thin air,
They vanish, until, off, you clear.

Then altogether, forget the weather,
We'll go a-birding, by hook or crook,
On recognition, we've done our homework,
So we'll get a tick in the book.

"You Are My Sunshine"

WEST COUNTRY BIRD-WATCHERS

We are happy birders, and we keep our lists,
Some people would call us Ornithologists,
Hope and expectation gives us all a kick,
Ever optimistic for that mega-tick.

Chorus — We don't care for twi . . . . . tching,
Sometimes miss the bus,
But sooner or later,
"It" will come to us.

We're from Taw and Torridge, down in the South West,
And the local birding is the very best,
Here, right on our doorstep, pickings can be rich,
Vagrants, rare and lovely, turn up in a ditch.

RSPB's famous, caring for bipeds,
They, like sev'ral Waders, thrive in Sandy Beds,
There are County Bird Clubs almost everywhere,
Members keeping records as they "stand and stare".

What's that in the bushes? Difficult to say,
It's a little brown job many yards away,
Nothing diagnostic can be seen at all,
And, of course, you've guessed it, it will make no call.

"Onward Christian Soldiers"

WHEN IT'S HALDON AND SAID, WHAT BETTER PLACE FOR THAT FIRST FINE FEARLESS RAPTOR

And did we meet in ancient pines,
Walking among those Haldon trees,
And was the Honey Buzzard up,
And searching for those wasps and bees,
And did the Goshawk thrill us too,
In gliding 'cross a cloudless sky,
And was the Raptor Viewpoint made
On Haldon's pleasant slopes nearby?

Bring me my bins of light alloy,
Bring me my telescope to zoom,
Bring me my notebook to record,
Bring me my waterproofs, there's room,
I shall eschew sedent'ry life,
And everything I'll have to hand,
And we shall get those Birdline ticks,
Should it mean trips across the land.

And when the year draws to a close,
The twelve months list we then shall add,
And we shall all be on our toes,
To reach two hundred or go mad,
A modest aim perhaps it is,
When plus three hundred can be on,
With hands on telephone and wheel,
Prepared to drive hither and yon.

"Jerusalem"

HIJACK THAT HERRING

Hijack that herring, the Tern's been not unseen,
Hijack that herring, the Bonxie's pursuit,
Skuas are lazy, let Terns do the fishing,
Then they're persuaded to give up the loot.

Even the Gannets are chased by these pirates,
At snatching their catch the Skua makes a stab,
Victim disgorges, releases its breakfast,
Mugging marine style, it's just splash and grab.

"Come Back to Erin"

PARODIES OF CHRISTMAS CAROLS

No.1 "Good things, wintertime"

Good things, wintertime, no doubt,
On the marsh at Isley,
Where the wildfowl hang about,
It's a life of Riley;
Ducks and Waders, Spoonbill, Geese,
They all make a brave show,
Who would ponder their decease?
Peregrine will *stoop*, so low.

In the pasture and the sod,
Where the Crows aren't stinted,
Eat dead creatures, all the bod,
Sharing with their kindred,
Magpies, Rooks too like their meat,
Have a varied diet,
Fruit and insects, sour or sweet,
Anything they'll try it.

So we Torridge birders sing,
We are near the action,
Kenwith, Isley, to mind spring,
Giving satisfaction,
In South West we've habitats
Suiting many species,
Sea-birds, Waders, Passerines,
We love them to pieces.

"Good King Wenceslas"

No.2 "Many Starlings foreigners are"

Many Starlings foreigners are,
Swelling numbers well above par,
Autumn flocking, roosting, docking,
They're not particular,
Oh, they fill ledges, and facade,
Huddling up so many a yard,
Gawking, squawking, neighbours baulking,
Settling down can be quite hard.

Sometimes there can be odd one out,
Eastern vagrant, a gadabout,
The Rose-coloured is no dullard,
But can discovery flout,
Oh, when it's in a thousand flock,
And you're trying to take stock,
You can miss it, every visit,
Not exactly a Peacock.

"We Three Kings of Orient Are"

No.3 "A Wader's in Danger"

A Wader's in danger, on estu'ry mud,
That Peregrine threatens, is it out for blood?
The Redshank are wary, they raise the alarm,
There is general panic, will one come to harm?

The Falcon is slowing, it comes in to land,
Another strike later is probably planned,
The shore-birds now settle, the mud they reclaim,
And hope pressing hunger won't help raptor's aim.

Low tide, in their hundreds, the birds they will feed,
Reacting to threats with all possible speed,
They all rise as one from nutritional mire,
In coastal location, the straits can be dire.

"Away in a Manger"

No.4 "Silent Night, Owly Night"

Silent Night, Owly Night,
Tawny one needs a bite,
Hunts the edge of the woodland so keen,
Quite soon rodents will be heard and seen,
Supper time is now here.

Owly sight, in the daylight,
Short-eared one, flapping flight,
Will collect where most voles can be found,
Quartering, searching hard, just above ground,
Or at ease on a post.

Owly sight, twilight or night,
The Barn one, oh so white,
Curdles the blood with its shrill piercing call,
Losing sites so their numbers they fall,
Species endangered it is.

Owly sight, daylight or night,
Little one, close up tight,
'Gainst the trunk of a tree, hard to see,
Or on the roof of a barn it might be,
Easily overlooked.

"Silent Night, Holy Night"

MISCELLANEOUS

SPRING SONNET TO PRESQU'ILE

There's plenty on offer down at Presqu'ile,
When it's migration time, say, in the Spring,
And there's so much coming north, on the wing;
Some trees, as yet unleaved, cannot conceal
Flycatchers, Warblers, Grosbeaks, they reveal,
The Woodpeckers' thumps in the forest ring,
Then your birding day will have everything,
Indeed what pastime could have more appeal?
Take a wander along the Marsh Boardwalk
Whence Caspian Terns, Blue Herons are seen,
With Pied-billed Grebes and Virginia Rails,
Whilst the Marsh Wren clings to a sedge's stalk;
Is the Bittern hid by the reed-bed screen?
And the Blue-winged Teal, by the dense cat-tails?

DUNGENESS

Now Dungeness, Kent is a place rather bleak,
But it has its good points if it's birds that you seek,
There are acres of shingle, and pebbles galore,
That the migrants they don't feel inclined to ignore,
The gravel pits hold varied birds through the year,
So whenever you go there'll be ticks, never fear,
Many hectares are owned by the RSPB,
It is somewhere for birding with great pedigree.

A hide and Observatory by the tidemark,
Where a sea-watch can yield species well worth remark,
Marine ones are noteworthy and hard to match,
Some time later there'll be Gulls and Terns on the Patch,
From the road, the ARC pit don't fail to observe,
A scrutiny keen it will always deserve.
The Stone Curlew's long gone, but that needn't detract,
You'll find something your records have hitherto lacked.

Past Boulderwall Farm, that is where you go in,
On a rough stony road through the scrub and the whin,
Traversing the track, like a coarse pebble beach,
It's the Centre, and it's Burrowes Pit that you reach,
The Pit is extensive with more than one hide,
You'll seldom watch there and be dissatisfied,
Now the Roseate Tern does in Summer appear,
Whilst the Med Gull is likely a family to rear.

Whatever the season there's something to see,
Most unlucky if everything's an absentee,
Come Autumn the Waders, so many, pass through,
With the chance of a rarity on its debut,
Assemblies in Winter, the fowl they abound,
When various Grebes, Ducks, and Divers are found,
And the Spring, in Reserve, or on coast will reward,
That's an optimum time, you should get a rich hoard.

BOUGH BEECH RESERVOIR

Set in the valley, below Ide Hill,
For birders it's worth a long vigil,
And gaps in your list you well might fill,
Rarities happen.

This, Western Kent's reserve aquatic,
Gets ornithologists ecstatic,
Some arrivals can be dramatic.
What will appear next?

Ospreys the area ornament,
With talons, on fishing they are bent,
On migration, north or south, through Kent,
Most welcome callers.

Resident nearby, in an oak copse,
Little Owl is seen as it hedge hops,
Or in the fork of a tree, it stops,
Can be elusive.

Little Ringed Plover, one to delight,
Sometimes a Barn Owl, near to twilight,
Fifty plus Eider, that was a sight,
Days to remember.

North Lake's where many a wader calls,
In the autumn as the level falls,
Studying Sandpipers never palls,
Shanks for the mem'ry.

With Grey Phalarope and Whooper Swan,
Little Tern, Wryneck, the list goes on,
A visit is a *sine qua non*,
Can't afford to miss.

ON REACHING AN ANNUAL TWO HUNDRED

Fight fatigue, fight fatigue,
Fight fatigue, onward,
Into the Marsh of Romney
Drive for two hundred;
So to a halt we ground,
Is there a Smew around?
And if so, can it be found?
To make two hundred.

Said to be, said to be,
Said to be westward,
The far end of Burrowes Pit,
Should make two hundred;
In that great raft of duck,
With just a bit of luck,
In, the towel, do not chuck,
Must get two hundred.

'Gainst the sun, 'gainst the sun,
'Gainst the sun, awkward,
But that must not halt the drive
On to two hundred,
Down from those pylons two,
Left of that post, you'll view
A small group of lovely Smew,
Score now two hundred.

Bonuswise, bonuswise,
Bonuswise, extra,
Denge Marsh then produced a goose,
Beyond conjecture,
Stayed to be clearly seen,
No runner, adult Bean,
Right there upon the scene,
Over two hundred.

DAVID BOAG
(or "Have you heard the Puffin Man?")

It was David Boag who told us,
A most entertaining talk,
Illustrated quite superbly,
With slides of that wonderful Auk.

He went to the island of Skomer,
To stay and get a good look,
And study the Puffin's lifestyle,
He's described it in a grand book.

Arriving in Spring from the seaward,
Taking burrows from rabbits,
But the Puffin doesn't copy
The previous owners' habits.

But one egg is laid in the tunnel,
After courtship quite unique,
Some trips round the bay together,
They, as it were, click with the beak.

He insinuated a camera,
Underground shutter he pressed,
We saw the egg, white and lonely,
There's not much semblance of a nest.

And we saw the chick, dark and fluffy,
Stuffed, a piscatory podge,
Some subterranean training,
Then nocturnal, it leaves the lodge.

Not content to stay on the island
At sea, David chased them miles,
And got some wonderful pictures,
Of Puffin submarine trials.

We recommend David most highly,
He talks in genial vein,
He's also a first-class lensman,
We hope that we'll see him again.

NOTHING LIKE SURE BIRDS

I must go down to the sea again, what a fascination it has,
Where the Oystercatchers, mussel snatchers gather there *en masse*,
Bills can be pointed or chiselled, diff'rent diet's no bar,
Avoiding harder shellfish when in the month there's an R.

I must go down to the sea again, and see Sand'ling without concern,
They'll chase a wave, and watch it cave, and will then dodge its return,
The sand beach is its larder, food's all swallowed, nothing's chewed,
Almost eating at the double, that's certainly fast food.

I must go down to the sea again, with all of the optical gear,
And all I ask is a good spring tide to push the Waders near,
When, watching the parade, some at ease, some at attention,
Suddenly they dismiss, look for Raptors in ascension.

I must go down to the sea again, though the Autumn wind can blow chill
For it's then that something special's found in estuary or pill
Storm driven, the avian compass vain, their goose is cooked,
Those unsuspecting migrants miss the holiday they'd booked.

KENWITH

Bideford patch where folks work hard,
And Waterfowl have stayed and thrived,
When visit those exotic Duck,
And Warblers too, it has arrived.

Fam'lies turn up with bread to feed,
Mallard which flock from far and wide,
Evident, at such times we see,
Children's delight, and *Mother's Pride*.

We say "Well done" to all concerned,
Kenwith's on conservation maps,
Where varied plumage cheers the eye,
And they've earned feathers in their caps.

BURSDON MOOR

A great place for wintering Raptors,
Other sites may improve on the score,
Now we've strong affection for Haldon,
But we certainly love Bursdon Moor.

Harriers are always attractive,
And Owls, also, are worth watching well,
When we want mercurial magic,
Only Merlin can cast the right spell.

CROSSBIRD
PUZZLES

CROSSBIRD NO. 1

"TRIOS"

The words required at the following lights:—
ACROSS — 2, 5, 13, 17, 23, 32, 39
DOWN — 1, 3, 5, 7, 14, 20, 25, 34
are fifteen names of birds divided into five Groups of three, designated Groups A, B, C, D, & E. The three birds in each Group are closely linked ornithologically. The twelve in Groups A to D are, with one exception, resident breeding species in the UK. The trio in Group E are hardly likely to be seen, genuinely wild, in the UK.

OTHER CLUES

ACROSS

1. with 41 across. American cousin to Group B. (4)
9. Aboriginal, as a member of Group E. (5)
10. Observing keenly as do members of Group C. (5)
11. Tasty morsel for Group A. (5)
15. Bird seen in same general area as Group A, though not tied to it! (4)
16. Athlete, as each of Group E needs to be. (6)
21. Coastal feature where Groups A & B may be found. (5)
24. Where Group C are at home. (5)
26. Members of Group B do, as do Group A to some extent; 15 across does. (4)
27. Failed possibly. But it's where you will succeed in finding Groups B & D, quite often! (6)
29. Golden food opportunity for Group A. (4)
35. Arboreal habitat for some of Groups C, D, & E. (5)
36. Nationality of criminal body snatcher whose accomplice's name is an anagram of one member of Group E. (5)
37. Features of all fifteen, but they do not fulfil the intended function for Group E. (5)
40. Surprise call of one of Group D! (3)
41. see 1 across.

DOWN

4. with 38 down. Group E's ability to fly has. (4)
6. East Anglian name for one of Group A, could seem to be! (4)
8. At which Group A excels. (6)
9. Just where to find members of Groups A & B, sometimes. (4)
12. Breastbone condition that applies to Group E. (6)
18. Try this English river. Those of Group A would like to. (4)
19. Element for all except Group E. (3)
22. These are what Group C uses to grasp. (6)
23. The call of some members of the same broad family as Group C. (3)
28. Generic name of one member of Group B. (6)
30. Generic name of each member of Group C. (5)
31. Familiar name for certain birds of the same family as Group D. (4)
32. English location where to find some members of Groups A, B, & C particularly. (4)
33. Populous place where several of Groups A to D can exist. (4)
38. see 4 down.

CROSSBIRD NO. 2

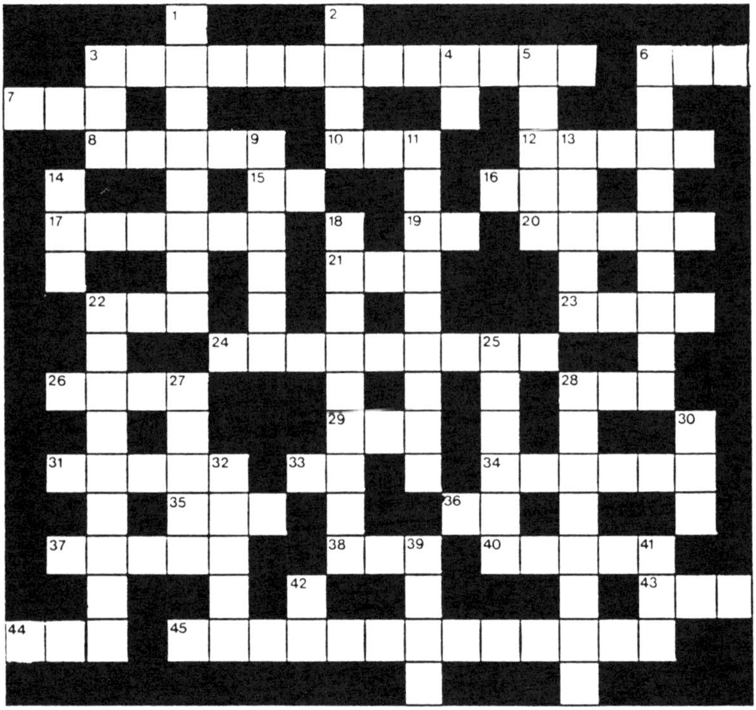

"THRUSHES AND FINCHES"

The words required at the following lights:—
ACROSS — 3 (two words 5, 8) 8, 17 see 23 across, 23 with 17 across, 29 see 37 across, 37 with 29 across.
DOWN — 11, 22, 30 with 39 down, 39 see 30 down
are the names of seven UK members of the Thrush family (Turdidae).
And the words required at the following lights:—
ACROSS — 22 with 35 across, 24, 26 see 30 down, 31, 40.
DOWN — 6, 18, 25, 30 with 26 across
are the names of eight UK members of the Finch family (Fringillidae). Two of these are uncommon.
The names at 23 across with 17 across, and at 18 down, are both plurals.
It will be seen that 19 across and 30 down are used twice!

OTHER CLUES

ACROSS

6. see 32 down.
7. Eggs are nearly egg-shape! (3)
10. North Country Crow. (3)
12. In the eighty-fourth one, of an old book, we read of the Swallow as a 9 down. (5)
15. see 33 across.
16. Could shelter a Shetland bird. (3)
19. see 36 across, and 4 down.
20. Very fast, screamer in fact! (5)
21. Crow losing tail, becoming bigger and legendary. (3)
28. One of the 45 across. (3)
33. With 42 down and 15 across, it is one of the 1 down. (6)
34. Food for the Oystercatcher? (6)
36. with 19 across, Bill the magistrate. (4)
38. Used on 45 across sometimes. (3)
43. With 14 down, Parrot can become a carnivore. (6)
44. Is out to catch, but can be mist! (3)
45. They provide food and shelter for many birds. (Two words 8, 5)

DOWN

1. Songsters, could be greenish. (8)
2. Enjoyed by Thrushes and Finches (4)
3. But no impediment to identification. (3)
4. With 19 across, One of the foreign 45 across. (4)
5. Osprey loses its head, upsets Ptarmigans. (5)
9. see 12 across.
13. To whom birds are grateful for 2 down. (5)
14. see 43 across.
27. Animal that flew higher than any bird. (5)
28. Thrushes and Finches are, keeping the family at home. (8)
32. With 6 across, Comprises three-quarters of a bird's element. (8)
41. Vetch of the bitter sort, puts an end to Waders. (3)
42. see 33 across.

CROSSBIRD NO. 3

"BAKER'S DOZEN"

The solutions to the following lights:—
ACROSS — 3 with 1 down, 20, 21, 26, 30, 34, 39.
DOWN — 1 see 3 across, 9, 12, 14, 15, 23, 29
are thirteen names of birds which can be divided into three groups of three and one group of four. The birds in each group are closely linked ornithologically. For convenience the groups of three are called A, B, and C, whilst the group of four is D. All thirteen birds may be seen in the UK. None is rare, though the breeding population of one is restricted. Non UK breeders comprise one of group B, one of group C and three of group D. Two names are in the plural, and four names each have two words.

OTHER CLUES

ACROSS

1. For two of Group A this is subterranean, for two of Group B it's arboreal, and for Groups C & D it's on Moorland, Tundra, Coast. (4)
6. Small stuff taken by Groups A & B. (3)
8. All will so immerse, some go deeper than others. (3)
10. Growth providing habitat for Group B. (5)
11. Just a trickle, might suit Group B. (6)
13. Crumbling Western Isle is an area where many of the thirteen might be seen. (5)
15. Natural Element of Groups A & C. (3)
16. The Rock variety can be found near Group D. (5)
18. Could be food for several of the thirteen. (3)
19. Is it a marsupial member of Group B? (6)
24. Erratic rude man to imitate a nursery Goose, and what all will do from time to time. (7)
27. Likely to be encountered by Group B, and swallowed. (3)
28. These are necessary for proper wing movements. (5)
29. Once it was decorated by robbing a member of Group B. (3)
31. Somerset area for Group B. (6)
36. Consumed, inside one of Group A! (3)
37. Cheshire feature for many of the thirteen. (3)
38. Wing feature common to all in Group D. (3)

DOWN

2. Marine creature of colour that Groups A & B might find paletteable! (5)
4. State of the tide to give best feeding opportunity for Groups B & D. (Three words 1, 3, 3)
5. All thirteen can take to this, some more readily than others. (3)
6. A habitat for Group B. (3)
7. Scientific name for N. American cousin of Group D. (Two words 8, 7)
17. Old name for wing. (5)
22. Applies to all thirteen, they will 24 across. (5)
25. Where jumpers are reared, they should attract Group B. (7)
32. Coastal feature of Orkney and Shetland where most of the thirteen can be found. (3)
33. Old meaning to what all thirteen can do, and pigs certainly do. (3)
35. Small bird not often seen in the company of any of the thirteen. (3)

CROSSBIRD NO. 4

"SANDPIPERS, WARBLERS AND BUNTINGS"

The words required at the following lights:—
ACROSS — 3, 26, 39
DOWN — 3, 34
are the names of five Sandpipers.
The words required at the following lights:—
ACROSS — 10, 17, 18, 23
DOWN — 16, 20
are the names of six Warblers.
And the words required at the following lights:—
ACROSS — 6 see 13 across, 13 with 6 across, 31, 35, 38
DOWN — 14, 35

are the names of six Buntings. The name at 13 across with 6 across is in the plural. In all the other sixteen cases it is only the adjectival part of the name of a Sandpiper, Warbler, or Bunting that is required.
The words "Sandpiper", "Warbler", and "Bunting" do not appear in the solutions.
The word at 13 across can also apply to a Nearctic Warbler!

OTHER CLUES

ACROSS

8. When doubled it's a Latin cousin of 19 down. (4)
9. They are the 29 across of a colourful visitor. (4)
12. Saw the Shearwater without this, which is uncommon. (4)
15. Botanical feature, could provide a perch for a small bird. (4)
21. In winter not to be seen here, this sea-bird. (4)
24. One was written about a 19 down species, French. (4)
27. Sick Raven tailed, not alive, but warm. (6)
29. All birds have one, and for a Sandpiper it can depend on the turn of the tide! (4)
33. Nothing French upset the headless Serin. (4)
36. Half Hemipode hopeless, confused. (4)
37. Against Greek, Martin loses title, agitated. (4)

DOWN

1. Behead a sea-bird, and get a Kittiwake. (5)
2. Top Osprey loses stoop, but gets a catch. (4)
4. Such a straw is a Yorkshire Reed Warbler. (5)
5. What the Carpal joints are sometimes called. (6)
6. Ducks not uncommonly, do this. (9)
7. Applies to most birds to some degree. (7)
11. Half a Latin Corncrake, not caught, but crowned. (3)
19. Scottish Jackdaw. (3)
22. That of a bird hides in the coverts. (3)
25. Animal tour in our absence moved to the best time of the day for birds. (7)
28. Strangely enough it's quite often a Blackbird. (6)
30. Miss by going round for fruit that many birds take. (3)
32. Characteristic of Great Tit . . . get away! (5)

CROSSBIRD NO. 5

"QUACKERS!"
DUCKS of all kinds.

ACROSS

3. A dabbler. (7)
10. with 26 across. A sea duck, scientifically. (6, 6)
11. British duck haunt. (3)
12. Rangy Teal are leaving, might be the seaweed. (6)
13. This bill's a sea duck. (3)
15. Andersen's young duck was, superlatively so! (7)

16. Merganser oiled, no green, no red, Wader Group left in confusion. (6)
17. Cricket duck. (3)
18. Yet diving Loon no novelty, got a Blue! (6)
19. with 20 across. Colour of Common Scoter drake. (5)
20. see 19 across.
21. Sea duck. (9)
23. with 33 down. Duck shooting must in Feb. (5)
25. Second element for a duck. (3)
26. see 10 across.
27. Tree that might provide shade for a Caribbean duck. (3)
30. Small watercourses that could attract Mallard. (6)
31. see 22 down.
32. Note, two ducks in the sticky stuff! (3)
34. When drakes can be in eclipse. (6)
35. British estuary duck haunt. (3)
36. Transatlantic Scaup. (6)
38. First Goosander in road, disturbed, bowing down. (7)

DOWN

1. When they do might be the best time to identify ducks. (3)
2. Sea duck. (4, 6)
4. The general family of Geese, Swans and Ducks. (8)
5. Another dabbler. (6)
6. Kind of Teal. (6)
7. A duck is this of course. (3)
8. Another dabbler. (8)
9. American coast where 2 down winters. (7)
14. Tossing about in the sea as ducks will. (9)
19. Where the Wildfowl Trust began. (10)
22. When its product is in 31 across there can be danger for ducks and other sea-birds. (8)
23. Another kind of Teal. (8)
24. Wildfowl refuge. (7)
28. Soundly afloat, and this of the duck type can keep your feet dry! (1, 5)
29. One who goes duck shooting. (6)
33. see 23 across.
37. What the French duck floats on. (3)

CROSSBIRD NO. 6

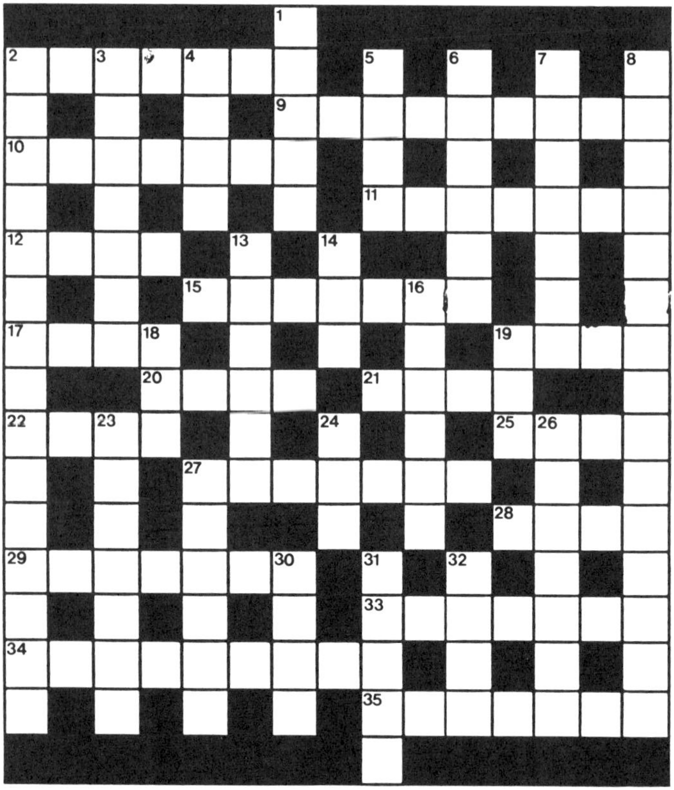

"WILD BIRD MIXTURE"

ACROSS

2. Many grounded Geese need guide in strong winds. (7)
9. Reformed rocker can still be a noisy one. (9)
10. with 28 across. Scientifically a Heron, ate large bat for a change. (Two words 7, 4)
11. Small birds with rodent tail. (7)
12. Travers' work with Rookery, bit of a farce. (4)
15. Moorland runner. (7)

17. Prolific sources of arboreous food. (4)
19. In luck, I win, but keep both feet on the ground! (4)
20. Twice I'm in front with my large bill. (4)
21. His Warbler is a visitor, partially! (4)
22. Short Crows. (4)
25. Staffordshire Finch, not transatlantic! (4)
27. Hirsute as a Reedling. (7)
28. see 10 across.
29. Appropriately Flycatchers in Northants. (7)
33. As the Albatross, far from land. (7)
34. Not the Port, but good place for water birds in Shropshire. (9)
35. From the Dark Continent e.g. Paradise Flycatcher. (7)

DOWN

1. Merited by "Kes" the Kestrel? (5)
2. Raw plantation spirit, colourful insecticide! (Two words 5, 10)
3. Makes crock go, over Scottish moors you'll see it. (7)
4. Cock Robin was, in the rhyme. (4)
5. Rough stuff but birds can take it. (4)
6. Tresco, Isles of Scilly, for this Sea Duck. (6)
7. I'm a hick but become a screamer in South America. (7)
8. Can be leaning perforce, but stooping is more likely with this one. (Two words 9, 6)
13. Indigenous prey for a catcher? (6)
14. Whence flew a Raven and a Dove. (3)
16. Dash ahead of alien, and be a high flier. (6)
18. with 19 down. Relative joins family Finch. (6)
19. see 18 down.
23. Several species of this bird are 35 across. (7)
24. Somerset Heron. (3)
26. Zoological includes reference to birds' eggs, of course. (7)
27. Right inside animal, outside on a bird, can have diagnostic colour. (6)
30. Set me in a certain direction to find a Sawbill. (4)
31. Bill of 24 is sometimes so described. (5)
32. In ornithological articles, refers to wings. (4)

CROSSBIRD NO. 7

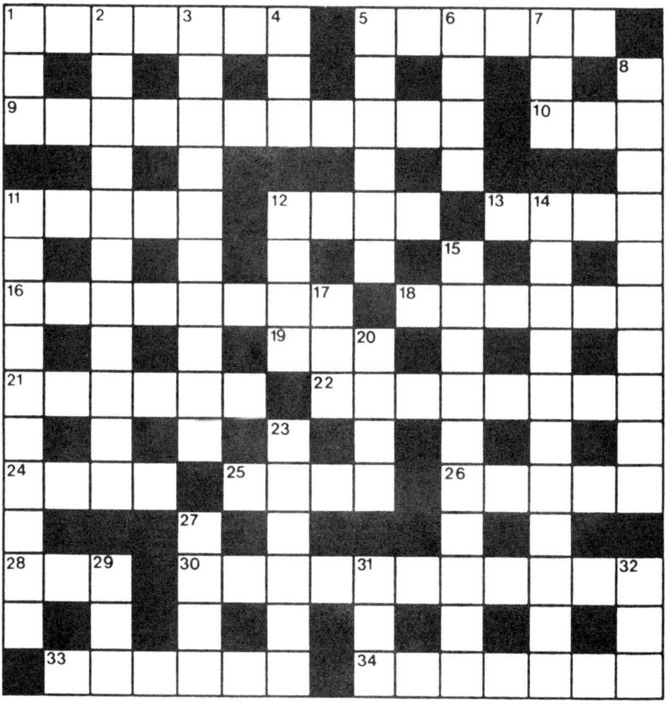

"FEATHERED BLEND"

ACROSS

1. This flapper hangs about. (7)
5. Surgeon out, loses direction, on the moors. (6)
9. Hawklike. New Captain is fiercer, no fears! (11)
10. Secretary Bird's elevenses. (3)
11. Restrain this wader. (5)
12. Southern Gull becomes a sea-duck. (4)
13. Raven appears in front of this cliff, on the N. E. Coast. (4)
16. Good Mother! Out and about after dark! (8)
18. Shropshire Flycatcher. (6)
19. Bill gets his pal back. (3)

21. Ron got out in the Tropical forest for this colourful bird. (6)
22. Moulted? (8)
24. Musical pipe for a Warbler or Bunting. (4)
25. Simple Diver. (4)
26. Some birds do when a construction job looms! (5)
28. Brood. (3)
30. Old Skua, subject of marine photo. (11)
33. Finch reduces in Lent. (6)
34. Foreign 8 down. (7)

DOWN

1. NZ Bird, found in park, easily recognised. (3)
2. "I will roar you as gently as any . . . ." (Shakespeare) (Two words 7, 4)
3. What Thrushes and Parrots can be guilty of. (10)
4. With an adult bird is a young one. (3)
5. Was golden this fowl. (6)
6. This bird is in a stove nest. (4)
7. "And the . . . . . Gulls crying." (Masefield) (3)
8. Christmas present game. (Two words 1, 9)
11. Mavis the vocalist. (Two words 4, 6)
12. Pen with an orange nib. (4)
14. I follow the saint in spirit, leading to the dovecot. (11)
15. Another name for one of the Warblers. (Two words 6, 4)
17. Colour of a barred Owl. (3)
20. Green Goose. (4)
23. Drum rolls back for this bird. (6)
27. Wing tip to wing tip. (4)
29. Parson begins tuition. (3)
31. This mouse is a small bird. (3)
32. Emulates, at first, but can't fly like other birds. (3)

CROSSBIRD NO. 8

"FLYING FARRAGO"

ACROSS

1. Old sailor killed this bird of good omen. (9)
5. Prepare to steal an egg. (5)
9. In the manner of a Crow. (6)
10. Confused Aussie Crow that is missing, in Tropical America. (8)
11. Might be withdrawn from a mud bank by a wader. (6)
14. A birder's record, hark! (4)
15. Reaches exalted nest unkempt and early. (7)
16. "In the wilderness build me a . . . ." (4)
18. Plurally held to get a singularly good view! (3)

19. "The . . . . appear on the earth, the time of singing of birds is come." (Song of Solomon) (7)
20. Written to Nightingale and Skylark, amongst others. (3)
21. "There I couch when . . . . . . do cry." (Shakespeare) (4)
24. Batman's easily combatant. (7)
26. This Raptor is a bit of a flier near the coast. (4)
28. Familiar fierce fish filcher from fliers. (6)
29. In advance of seeing it, you might hear it "going back!" (8)
31. Screech-Owl plays tricks. (6)
32. Goose of Ancient Rome. (5)
33. Scalped aquiline emblem! (Two words 4, 5)

DOWN

1. Some Chateau Dubonnet for the great American ornithologist: (7)
2. Swan sick, web awry. (7)
3. Cliff dweller yet it's dizzy. (6)
4. What parent bird removes from the nest. (3)
6. Ring this, it can make a loud call. (5)
7. Finch looks for weather signals, can be red, green, yellow. (9)
8. Bit of a bloomer, but a bird will accept it. (10)
12. Skylarks waxed in total, no. not down. (10)
13. Turn Plovers into stew and pie. (7)
17. Suffering owner died, poor duck provided a duvet. (9)
22. Polish corps, smart, we hear berets are favoured! (7)
23. Tends to be more prominent on juvenile plumage. (7)
25. Sally from Hawks or Tiercels. (6)
27. Where Eagles rear. (5)
30. Partly like a Parrot. (3)

CROSSBIRD NO. 9

"ORNIGRAMS"

With one exception, each clue includes a bird name, and also the letters, in no particular order, which make up the required solution (nothing to do with birds). The exception is 12 down where the solution is the name of a bird.

Each clue also contains a hint as to how the necessary letters can be found!

EXAMPLE — "Magpies are danger, cost nests; garden menace persists, *must go*. They are wicked." (5).

Removing the letters in "garden menace persists" from "Magpies are danger, cost nests" there remain the letters "A, G, O, S, T" which make the word "GOATS", a word which can be applied to wicked folk. So the solution is "GOATS"!

ACROSS

1. Moving succession of Martins, E.N.E., nine passed. (6)
4. Pallid Harriers raced her, going E., are shrill, rapid; scorched. (7)
9. Upper-class Surf Scoter without crest, reddish. (6)
10. And in the middle, the Flamingo, almost gone away. (8)
11. Dead Pintail, no diet for a Knight. (7)
13. Vireos shot, fragments. Too, too much. (7)
14. Wanting nuts, pelagic Raptor hunts about rocks. (14)
16. Drawing power, ace Stint travels without young driver. (14)
20. Godwit, Northern Limosa alighted, unsettled, gives rise to a curse. (7)
22. Between ourselves, our Sabine's lacking in energy. (3, 4)
23. The Toucan in Ireland, or in the end, lost re navigation. (8)
24. Alas, torn Lapwing hasn't grown. (6)
25. He paints Sheldrake, out in the parks, tied up. (7)
26. Egret ails on, start of a temperature, lies off colour. (6)

DOWN

1. Their moor; Great Snipe gather no more, I go looking, it's a blow. (6)
2. The green on Fulmar, harmless, no additive, brilliant. (9)
3. The loud Curlew Sandpiper, not Purple, cold white in parts. (7)
5. Capital protection, he'd conserved Shearwaters, restored when disappeared. (11)
6. A Ruff, its collar washy so soon as colours lost on way out, was flashy. (7)
7. An elegant Ox-bird on Tees, take off. Abandon rest, get on, away from home. (5)
8. Teal asleep? Gone pale, will get a nap, under plant. (6)
12. Harmonious subject in wood, carved in light gean. (11)
15. Dunlin type on coast, "Plenty, no missing them" Warden said. (9)
16. Firing at Game in field, fled E. away. (6)
17. See flier, Sula Bassana? Unable, far off, annoys. (7)
18. Misty; are Terns blue when trees can't be seen? (7)
19. Scarcest Eagle, see crag, flown its stronghold. (6)
21. A ring-ousel! Honest? — No! He's ignorant, worthy of contempt. (5)

CROSSBIRD NO. 10

"CROSSBARD"

A.The words required at the following lights are the names of Characters in Shakespeare's Plays:—
ACROSS — 1, 4, 10, 17, 25, 27, 28, 30, 31
DOWN — 1, 4, 12, 16, 18, 23
4 down is a Character's alternative title. The clues at the above-mentioned lights, when solved, will give the names of the Plays which feature the required Characters. Once the Play has been found, study the Dramatis personae to find the name that fits any particular light. Each clue contains the name of a bird mentioned in that particular Play. All the letters needed to spell out the name of a Play are in the clue,

and are consecutive.
EXAMPLE:— Look at that Finch, foolish, mad, see it drumming, rams tree. (6)
SOLUTION:— . . . . sh, mad, see it drumming, ram . . ." which are the letters to spell out "A MIDSUMMER NIGHT'S DREAM", and the Character (six letters) could be "Quince".

A. "Character" clues

ACROSS

1. There's a Duck in that pool, the lower one. (6)
4. Small and dark, it was they thought, a melanistic Sparrow. (8)
10. The Fowl, we assume, roam free, run about. (8)
17. About that Goose, Jethro wired me, "Verify Snow species." (3, 4, 8)
25. Great Eagle over apartment, they told me Janitor euphoric. (6)
27. Rare Gull at Barmouth, not on sea, I'm forced to say. (8)
28. Alternatively, there's a Dove on ivy wall, without. (6)
30. Crow takes gut, Chough abandon it moodily. (8)
31. The Martlets look smart, bathe, no doubt, each morning. (6)

DOWN

1. Will the Owl's catch be a mouse? (6)
4. That Kite, a male, watch him, athletic, twisting tail. (6, 2, 7)
12. There's Capon, get hart, hern, fruit, honey, kitchen's ready. (4)
16. Nightingales in left hawthorn, might see eventually. (9)
18. Read about Hawk, watch raptor wing in the sky, text has got it right. (4)
23. Phoenix burnt to ashes, faint not, mounts again. (5)

B. The words required at the remaining lights appear in Shakespeare, though they are not necessarily "Shakespearian". Each of these remaining clues contains a bird's name, and also, the letters, once again consecutive, which go to make up the solution.
EXAMPLE:— "It's hard to find a silent GOLDCREST in a tree."
SOLUTION:— "Gent", "Got", "Stain", or "Taint" etc!

B. Other clues

ACROSS

8. The scoundrel ran over four CHUKAR — tragic. (3)
9. Remember NUTCRACKER party in the conifers, those ten. (6)
11. Cat annoys our SARUS, pursues it, grabs it. (6)
13. Don't applaud SKUA, studying sea-birds too closely, there will be turmoil (1, 4)
14. A robber HARRIER startles the rabbit which hops away. (4)
20. In company they came, TURNSTONE methodically salvaging. (4)
22. A neat STONECHAT perched, along the country path. (5)
29. You can spot RAVENS at a rubbish tip. (3)

DOWN

2. In their amours, MERGANSERS more raucous, can give offence. (9)
3. Watch that sea area where SCOTER scattered. (5)
5. It was a December DOWITCHER, dawn arrival, surrounded by other Waders. (5)
6. There flies SHRIKE, a warning to the insects in the Hebrides. (5)
7. Simple for OSPREYS really, making a catch. (4)
13. See that young male BUZZARD lolling in the nest, victim of fratricide. (4)
15. Looks a bit buffo, FLAMINGO feeding away. (3)
17. Clamorous NIGHTJARS, nocturnal, of course, and native. (3)
19. Presence of JAYS will have an influence on the number of acorns. (4)
21. Even the poorest KINGFISHER takes some beating, don't you agree? (6)
24. A bird called, NUTHATCH, gave forth a musical sound. (5)
25. Within a foot — THRUSH; Snail's had it. Eaten with relish. (5)
26. ROOKS battered STARLING, severe wound inflicted. (4)

CROSSBIRD SOLUTIONS

CROSSBIRD SOLUTIONS

CROSSBIRD No. 1 — "TRIOS"

Across: 1.So 2.Emu 5.Kestrel 9.Maori 10.Eying 11.Elver 13.Peregrine 15.Knot 16.Runner 17.Coot 21.Inlet 23.Merganser 24.Aerie 26.Wade 27.Afield 29.Orfe 32.Water-Rail 35.Sylva 36.Irish 37.Wings 39.Moorhen 40.Caw 41.Ra
Down: 1.Smew 3.Magpie 4.Go 5.Kiwi 6.Smee 7.Raven 8.Diving 9.Mere 12.Ratite 14.Goosander 18.Test 19.Air 20.Crow 22.Talons 23.Mew 25.Merlin 28.Fulica 30.Falco 31.Daws 32.Wash 33.Town 34.Rhea 38.Ne

(Group A — Merganser, Smew, Goosander. Group B — Water-Rail, Coot, Moorhen. Group C — Peregrine, Merlin, Kestrel. Group D — Magpie, Crow, Raven. Group E — Emu, Kiwi, Rhea)

CROSSBIRD No. 2 — "THRUSHES AND FINCHES"

Across: 3.Black Redstart 6.Gen 7.Ova 8.Robin 10.Dob 12.Psalm 15.En 16.Geo 17.Ousels 19.Ak 20.Swift 21.Roc 22.Sis 23.Ring 24.Crossbill 26.Poll 28.Ash 29.Ear 31.Serin 33.Ga 34.Native 35.Kin 36.Be 37.Wheat 38.Saw 40.Twite 43.Rap 44.Net 45.Woodland Trees
Down: 1.Warblers 2.Seed 3.Bar 4.Te 5.Rypes 6.Goldfinch 9.Nester 11.Blackbird 13.Sower 14.Tor 18.Grosbeaks 22.Stonechat 25.Linnet 27.Laika 28.Altrices 30.Red 32.Nitro 39.Wing 41.Ers 42.Rd

CROSSBIRD No. 3 — "BAKER'S DOZEN"

Across: 1.Nest 3.Gan 6.Fry 8.Dip 10.Typha 11.Runnel 13.Lewis 15.Sea 16.Pipit 18.Dab 19.Boomer 20.Bittern 21.Manx Shearwaters 24.Maunder 26.Dunlin 27.Asp 28.Radii 29.Hat 30.Scaup 31.Levels 34.Egret 36.Ate 37.Dee 38.Bar 39.Knot
Down: 1.Net 2.Sepia 4.A Low Ebb 5.Air 6.Fen 7.Calidris Pusilla 9.Purple Sandpiper 12.Little Stint 14.Scoter 15.Storm Petrel 17.Penne 22.Nomad 23.Eiders 25.Ranaria 29.Heron 32.Voe 33.Sty 35.Tit

(Group A — Storm Petrel, Gannet, Manx Shearwaters. Group B — Bittern, Egret, Heron. Group C — Scaup, Scoter, Eiders. Group D — Purple Sandpiper, Little Stint, Knot, Dunlin)

CROSSBIRD No. 4 — "SANDPIPERS, WARBLERS AND BUNTINGS"

Across: 3.Western 6.Hammers 8.Pica 9.Bees 10.Grey 12.Rare 13.Yellow 15.Axil 17.Garden 18.Dusky 21.Tern 23.Pallas's 24.Poem 26.Green 27.Ardent 29.Diet 31.Little 33.Rien 35.Corn 36.Demi 37.Anti 38.Ortolan 39.Spotted
Down: 1.Annet 2.Prey 3.White-rumped 4.Small 5.Elbows 6.Hybridise 7.Migrant 11.Rex 14.Lapland 16.Lanceolated 19.Kae 20.Sardinian 22.Ear 25.Matinal 28.Albino 30.Err 32.Trait 34.Least 35.Cirl

CROSSBIRD No. 5 — "QUACKERS!"

Across: 3.Gadwall 10.Aythya 11.Ayr 12.Tangly 13.Saw 15.Ugliest 16.Limosa 17.Nil 18.Indigo 19.Sab 20.Le 21.Goldeneye 23.Ce 25.Air 26.Marila 27.Ita 30.Bourns 31.Transit 32.Goo 34.Autumn 35.Dee 36.Lesser 38.Adoring
Down: 1.Fly 2.Surf Scoter 4.Anatidae 5.Wigeon 6.Laysan 7.She 8.Garganey 9.Pacific 14.Weltering 19.Slimbridge 22.Oilfield 23.Cinnamon 24.Arundel 28.A Board 29.Punter 33.Ase 37.Eau

CROSSBIRD No. 6 — "WILD BIRD MIXTURE"

Across: 2.Gaggles 9.Corncrake 10.Egretta 11.Titmice 12.Nook 15.Harrier 17.Oaks 19.Kiwi 20.Ibis 21.Savi 22.Daws 25.Nope 27.Bearded 28.Alba 29.Cobwebs 33.Pelagic 34.Ellesmere 35.African
Down: 1.Oscar 2.Green Woodpecker 3.Gorcock 4.Late 5.Grit 6.Scoter 7.Kamichi 8.Peregrine Falcon 13.Native 14.Ark 16.Elanet 18.Sis 19.Kin 23.Waxbill 24.Ern 26.Oologic 27.Breast 30.Smew 31.Spear 32.Alar

CROSSBIRD No. 7 — "FEATHERED BLEND"

Across: 1.Kestrel 5.Grouse 9.Accipitrine 10.Asp 11.Stint 12.Smew 13.Scar 16.Nightjar 18.Miller 19.Neb 21.Trogon 22.Deplumed 24.Reed 25.Loon 26.Weave 28.Sit 30.Pomatorhine 33.Linnet 34.Tinamou
Down: 1.Kea 2.Sucking Dove 3.Repetition 4.Let 5.Guinea 6.Oven 7.Sea 8.A Partridge 11.Song Thrush 12.Swan 14.Columbarium 15.Willow Wren 17.Red 20.Bean 23.Motmot 27.Span 29.Tui 31.Tit 32.Emu

CROSSBIRD No. 8 — "FLYING FARRAGO"

Across: 1.Albatross 5.Poach 9.Dawish 10.Curassow 11.Buckie 14.List 15.Extends 16.Nest 18.Bin 19.Flowers 20.Ode 21.Owls 24.Bantams 26.Erne 28.Bonxie 29.Moorcock 31.Strick 32.Anser 33.Bald Eagle
Down: 1.Audubon 2.Bewick's 3.Tystie 4.Sac 6.Ousel 7.Crossbill 8.Breadcrumb 12.Exaltation 13.Peewits 17.Eiderdown 22.Waxwing 23.Speckle 25.Sortie 27.Eyrie 30.Kea

CROSSBIRD No. 9 — "ORNIGRAMS"

Across: 1.Stream 4.Charred 9.Rufous 10.Halftime 11.Paladin 13.Shivers 14.Petrographical 16.Attractiveness 20.Malison 22.Sub Rosa 23.Nautical 24.Plaint 25.Leashed 26.Orange
Down: 1.Stripe 2.Refulgent 3.Asunder 5.Head-scarves 6.Raffish 7.Exile 8.Teasel 12.Nightingale 15.Custodian 16.Aiming 17.Assails 18.Nebular 19.Castle 21.Louse

CROSSBIRD No. 10 — "CROSSBARD"

Across: 1.Bianca (OTHELLO) 4.Polonius (HAMLET) 8.Cur 9.Number 10.Isabella (MEASURE FOR MEASURE) 11.Usurps 13.A Dust 14.Herb 17.Sir John Falstaff (THE MERRY WIVES OF WINDSOR) 20.Meet 22.State 25.Tybalt (ROMEO AND JULIET) 27.Timandra (TIMON OF ATHENS) 28.Orsino (WHAT YOU WILL)* 29.Rot 30.Benedick (MUCH ADO ABOUT NOTHING) 31.Hecate (MACBETH)

* "WHAT YOU WILL" is alternative title to "TWELFTH NIGHT"

Down: 1.Banquo (MACBETH) 2.Armourers 3.Acres 4.Prince of Denmark (HAMLET) 5.Orbed 6.Isles 7.Sear 12.Peto (KING HENRY THE FOURTH, PART ONE) 13.Abel 15.Off 16.Katharina (THE TAMING OF THE SHREW) 17.Son 18.Hume (KING HENRY THE SIXTH, PART TWO) 19.Sway 21.Stroke 23.Timon (TIMON OF ATHENS) 24.Tuned 25.Tooth 26.Stab